THE GOOD FIGHT

SHIRLEY CHISHOLM

THE GOOD FIGHT

AMISTAD
An Imprint of HarperCollinsPublishers

HarperCollins books may be purchased for educational, business, or sales promotional use. For information, please email the Special Markets Department at SPsales@harpercollins.com.

FIRST HARPERCOLLINS PAPERBACK PUBLISHED IN 2022

Library of Congress Cataloging-in-Publication Data is available upon request.

ISBN 978-0-06-316082-8

22 23 24 25 26 LSC 10 9 8 7 6 5 4 3 2 1

To Conrad Chisholm, my devoted husband

CONTENTS

PREFACE

ONE OF THE most dismaying aspects of politics and public life in America today is the increasingly closed nature of the entire political process, particularly at the highest level. We hear much these days about the growing power of the Presidency at the expense of Congress, the lack of White House communication with the public, the virtual end of Presidential press conferences, and the secret bargaining and trading of favors in the back rooms of the powerful—all of which have repelled many people in the country. The low voter turnout in the November 1972 elections was a disturbing barometer of the air of apathy and resignation which permeates the nation's political atmosphere in this new year, a terribly unhealthy sign in a democracy.

Sorrow over the deaths of two former Presidents and somber relief over the apparent halt in our massive military intervention in Southeast Asia do not seem enough to enable us to stop and blink and perhaps turn our eyes from the past—so much of which has shocked and confused Americans—in hopes of starting anew and refocusing our hopes and energies toward the urgent needs of our nation.

Yet there are nonetheless positive undercurrents coursing through the lifeblood of America. A strong economic performance seems imminent, hopefully promising more jobs. The recent Supreme Court decision on abortions gives me confidence that there are indeed men of reason and basic goodwill who are prepared to make terribly difficult and profound social and moral decisions despite sharp and highly emotional opposition. Furthermore, the election of a Democratic Congress in 1972 indicates to me that most Americans want a counter to the administration and have not forgotten those humane, progressive values which some feared were lost forever as our technological society rolled on.

In response to public demand, more light is being shed on our political process—on campaign financing, on convention delegate selection, and on Congressional committee operations. The recent decision by a Democratic caucus of the House to reform the seniority system may well have a significant impact on the ability of the House to respond more quickly and effectively to local and national problems.

I ran for the Presidency in order to crack a little more of the ice which in recent years has congealed to nearly immobilize our political system and demoralize people. I ran for the Presidency, despite hopeless odds, to demonstrate sheer will and refusal to accept the status quo.

It seems to me that a Presidential candidate can open the door a bit farther by discussing openly and frankly what transpired during his or her campaign—the pressures, the conflicts, the fears, the double crosses, the financial costs—while the campaign is fresh in the public mind and before the candidate reaches that autumnal time of life when the traditional memoir may be deemed suitable.

I therefore freely give my impressions of events and personalities as I perceived them during the 1972 Presidential primary campaigns. In so doing, I hope the public may better understand this grueling, often bewildering phase of our election system. Some readers may find their worst fears confirmed; others may feel compelled to participate themselves in some future campaign. Either way I feel that such a book may play a useful role in my continuing efforts to shake up our system.

February 1973, S.C.

ACKNOWLEDGMENTS

Grateful acknowledgment for assistance in the preparation of this book is due to Lee Hickling for research and editing aid and to Tracy Simmons for typing the manuscript.

To Wesley McD. Holder for his unswerving loyalty and determination on behalf of my political efforts—a political tactician with keen insight and the capacity to get the job done.

THE GOOD FIGHT

I.

The Nomination

IT WAS STRANGE that some of the people screaming the loudest were Wallace delegates with long red, white and blue neckties. One little white man kept jumping up and down; he didn't stop during the ten minutes it took for my acceptance speech. Little of the enthusiasm spread to the rostrum, though. Party chairman Larry O'Brien and the other officers at the Democratic National Convention in July, 1972, were impassive. It was an odd contrast; I noticed it fleetingly as I walked to the microphone.

There was no speech prepared. I didn't need one, because there was only one thing for me to say: "Brothers and sisters! At last I've reached this spot!" I don't remember my exact words. There are tape recordings somewhere, probably, for anyone who thinks the exact words matter. The placards waved, a band played, the hall was a stormy beach with waves made of people dressed in all colors, and their shouts were like the noise of an ocean. I had never seen a national convention session before except on television. State ones, yes. But the only convention I had gone to was the 1968 one in Chicago, and that was neither as a candidate nor as a delegate; when the session was nearly over I went to attend a meeting of the Democratic National Committee.

As I left my trailer behind the hall in Miami, surrounded by a ring of Secret Service men, I felt no excitement. Backstage, watching the scene on a television set until it was time to go on, I was still calm. But now this huge room was pulsing and jumping at me, so much more than I had expected. How long it went on, I could never tell. Even when I began to speak, they never really quieted down. If you had just landed from the moon, you might have thought that I was the convention's choice, not just a preliminary to the main event. I tried to focus on something and get myself together. People were leaving their seats, pushing through the chairs to the aisle below the speakers' platform, where I stood behind a huge-seeming lectern. Almost everybody was applauding and cheering—everybody except some of the McGovern delegates, who had contented themselves with a few claps. What I noticed most were the older black men and women. Some were crying, and their faces were so full of joy that they looked in pain. I thought I could read their lives' experiences in their faces at that instant, and I know what it was they felt. For a moment they really believed it: "We have overcome!"

What I said that night was that most people had thought I would never stand there, in that place, but there I was. All the odds had been against it, right up to the end. I never blamed anyone for doubting. The Presidency is for white males. No one was ready to take a black woman seriously as a candidate. It was not time yet for a black to run, let alone a woman, and certainly not for someone who was both. Someday . . . but not yet. Someday the country would be ready. Those were the things I had been told, everywhere I went for ten months, even before I announced officially that I was a candidate, and everywhere I was asked the same question: "But, Mrs. Chisholm—are you a *serious* candidate?" Each time, trying not to lose patience, I explained, and tonight I was explaining again.

Of course my candidacy had no chance. I had little money and no way of raising the funds it takes to run for high office. I had no big party figures supporting me. To the extent that they noticed me at all, the movers and shakers wished only that I would go away. A wild card, a random factor that might upset some detail of their plans, an intruder into the *real* contest among the white male candidates. Their response was ridicule—in private, not in public, because a gentleman doesn't make fun of a lady and a politician doesn't want to risk losing the black vote. But their attitude came through clearly: treat her with respect, but of course you don't have to take her seriously. If they ever wondered why I was running, their explanation was usually "Chisholm is on an ego trip."

So I did not devote my acceptance speech to a discussion of "the issues." I had discussed the issues before. People hear about the issues from every politician who gets up on a stump. They've quit listening to the traditional speeches with the traditional promises. "Fellow Americans, these are the great issues we must face. Fellow Americans, this is what I will do for you if you elect me." So what's new?

Who are you, and where are you coming from? Those are the questions people want to hear answered now. The old routine worked for a long, long time, but its time is done. I had no promises to make anyway, because I was not about to be the nominee. I had something more important to explain: why I was there. I'm still explaining it.

I ran because someone had to do it first. In this country everybody is supposed to be able to run for President, but that's never been really true. I ran *because* most people think the country is not ready for a black candidate, not ready for a woman candidate. Someday . . .

It was time in 1972 to make that someday come and, partly through a series of accidents that might never recur, it seemed to me that I was the best fitted to try. Once I was in the campaign, I had to stay all the way to the end, all the way to that night at the convention. Nothing less would have shown that I was "a serious candidate." If there had been only ten delegates ready to vote for me on the first ballot, instead of more than 150, I would still have stuck it out. The next time a woman runs, or a black, a Jew or any-one from a group that the country is "not ready" to elect to its highest office, I believe he or she will be taken seriously from the start. The door is not open yet, but it is ajar.

II.

After 1968

SENATOR HUBERT H. Humphrey might easily have been elected President in 1968. If about 1.5 percent of the votes in California and Illinois and only about 1 percent in New Jersey had shifted to him, those states with their 83 electoral votes would not have fallen to Richard M. Nixon. Humphrey would have won by 274 electoral votes to 228. Even without New Jersey he would have won by 22 electoral votes. Had he carried California and New Jersey but not Illinois, he would still have won by 4. The election was lost because too many voters stayed home, unwilling to cast a ballot for either candidate. Humphrey lost because he had supported President Lyndon B. Johnson on the Vietnam war and Mayor Richard Daley of Chicago on the police riot during the 1968 Democratic convention. The figures leave no doubt of it, in my mind. Of course, election returns are like the daily advice in a newspaper astrology column: everyone can find there whatever it is he wants to see. It is also possible to prove from the 1968 returns that Humphrey would have won if George Wallace had not been in the race, or that Nixon would have won even more decisively if Wallace had not been in it. It is possible to conclude almost anything, because we do not know very much about what goes on in a voter's head behind the curtains of a polling booth. Interpretation of the returns tells one more about the interpreter, I suppose, than it does about the returns. But the figures are there: Humphrey lost California's 40 votes by 3.1 percent, Illinois' 26 by 2.9 percent and New Jersey's 17 by 2.1 percent; and Nixon won 301 to 191. I choose to feel that Humphrey lost because he represented a Democratic Party that stood in the minds of youth for a hateful war, and because he did not win the allegiance of blacks and other minority voters to the extent that he, perhaps, deserved.

Leave the young voters aside for a moment; blacks make up between 15 and 20 percent of the United States population, and other racial minorities bring the total to nearly 30 percent. Minorities are numerous in cities of the three crucial states I named—California, Illinois and New Jersey. Their votes could have made the difference. Humphrey, I know, did well in black voting districts—among *registered* voters. But blacks in particular, and racial minorities in general, are the most under-registered part of the population. They do not vote because they see no salvation for them in either political party or candidate. They know that the parties represent the white majority, and that they are not true participants in the political process; all that the candidates want from them is a vote. So, quite pardonably, they tend to refuse to play such a demeaning role.

If ever a Presidential candidate's record qualified him for the support of blacks and other minorities, Humphrey's did. He was a civil rights advocate in the 1940s, long before it was a popular position, and he did more than talk; he went to the mat for equal rights at party conventions and in the Senate. Few if any white politicians are in his league as an ardent and sincere advocate of civil rights. There is no doubt that he deserved better from the people he had fought for than he got in the 1968 election. For that matter, he probably deserved more support than he received from the anti-war voters, young and old; a decent and peace-loving man, he would in all likelihood have put a much speedier end to the Southeast Asian war than did the victor in the contest. But this is exactly the point: one has to deal in politics not with reality *per se,* but with reality as it is perceived by voters, through clouds of distortion, simplification, prejudices and misinformation. Humphrey was looked on by anti-war voters as a crony of LBJ and Dick Daley; and to minority-group voters, particularly younger ones, he appeared to be just another white politician—nowhere near the sympathetic, compelling figure that Robert F. Kennedy had been, although (in all honesty) Kennedy had far less to show in the way of genuine, sustained effort in the minorities' cause. The point is that these groups stayed home because they saw no gain in participating in the electoral process; there was nothing in it for them. It was a crooked game, where heads you win and tails I lose.

My point is that Humphrey could have won if he and the Democratic Party had appeared only slightly, ever so slightly (a matter of a few percentage points) more credible to some of the groups of voters who had become disillusioned with the processes of representative government, or who (in the case of many blacks) had little or no faith in those processes to start with. That he did not manage to do so was a deplorable event, and it has, I believe, changed the history of this nation for the worse.

So these groups stayed away from the polls on Election Day, 1968, and their absence was decisive, because the old alignments were changing. The South was no longer solid, and the coalition that had made the Democrats a majority party for more than half a century was crumbling. A few people understood what was going on before the 1968 election; in the wake of it, there could be no doubt. Victory for the Democrats in 1972 was going to depend on a rather radical realignment of voting groups; to hope to restore the coalition that had elected Franklin D. Roosevelt, Harry S. Truman, and John F. Kennedy was not realistic. But the new shape of things remained unclear. The more some of the professionals and intellectuals thought about it, the more they began to wonder whether the end of the two-party system as they had known it was not in sight.

The full picture with all its details need not concern us;

the point I want to develop is that one of the elements of
the Democratic coalition that was falling away was the racial minority groups, the blacks, Indians, Puerto Ricans and
other citizens discriminated against because of the color of
their skins or their language differences. The position of
white ethnic minorities is an entirely different question, although there may be a few similarities. But blacks and the
other racial minorities were beginning more and more to
rebel at their role as captives of the Democrats, or as it has
been beautifully put, "tenants" in the party. "Where else can
they go?" the white politicians asked smugly. And it certainly seemed true that they had nowhere else to go, as the
first term of the Nixon administration unrolled: backtrack-
ing and waffling on school desegregation; cutbacks in job
programs; cutbacks in education; hostility to school lunch
and food stamp programs. "You don't solve problems by
throwing money at them," counseled Daniel Patrick Moyni-
han, the same Nixon adviser who achieved a kind of immor-
tality by coining the phrase "benign neglect." Indeed, it was
clear that no problems were going to be solved with money
by this administration; unemployment mounted until it
reached 15 percent or more in entire cities and counties, and
triple that in the black and Chicano districts. Urban housing
problems were "attacked" with programs that bankrupted
the poor and enriched speculators. The record of the Nixon
administration on minorities and poor people generally was
one of cruel inaction, punctuated with instances of outright
oppression.

Certainly, the Democrats had no reason to fear that the black vote and that of the other minorities would desert to the Republican Party. The party's white leaders could certainly sit back and count on the minorities for 1972; no great consideration needed to be given them, because they could easily be made to understand that, once again, the Democratic candidate would be for them the lesser evil.

Exactly who the party's leader would be was at that time far from settled—whether a traditional Democratic liberal like Humphrey or Senator Edmund S. Muskie of Maine, or a more mod candidate like Senator George S. McGovern of South Dakota, former Senator Eugene McCarthy or that recent convert Mayor John V. Lindsay of New York. There were even darker horses in the field. It was clear, as the 1972 primaries drew nearer, that they would be crowded ones. Not only was the glut of candidates bewildering but the party machinery also was undergoing some novel changes. One lesson had been learned from the 1968 defeat: there would have to be some way to attract the allegiance of the newly important youth bloc (there would be several million voters under eighteen in 1972, thanks to a new Constitutional amendment), and the increasingly independent and militant women's vote had to be considered; either one might be decisive. The minorities, too, were not going to be content with token representation any longer. A reform commission pondered these and other problems and came up with a radical reorganization of the rules by which the national party constituted itself and managed its business, particularly that of nominating a President. The new rules made it likely that there would be more black delegates than ever before at the 1972 nominating convention, by a wide margin, and more women delegates, and probably more young ones of whatever color or sex. It was little short of a revolutionary change—on paper. The 1968 defeat, and the specter of another in 1972, had jolted the Democrats into a healthy reaction; they were making a sincere effort to open up the party to all kinds of people, old and young, white and black, men and women. It seemed possible that this would be a new kind of campaign and a different kind of convention, with no more smoke-filled rooms where deals by a few insiders decided the important questions. The phrase was "the new politics."

But the new politics, promising as it looked at first, turned out to have one important thing in common with the older type—it was white men's politics. Blacks, other minorities and women were not in it on policy-making levels. No more than the older leaders did the "new politicians" understand the soul and psyche of the black person. They still saw white men naturally dominant in any kind of movement toward social amelioration. They were still, at best, at the stage of tokenism. And like older politicians, of whatever party, they still saw politics, and particularly Presidential politics, as the business of men. Of course, the candidates named "minority coordinators" to help them corral the black vote and set up "women's divisions" to appeal to the feminist vote. But these were second- and third-level posts, subordinates, order-takers and errand-runners. Where were the blacks, Puerto Ricans, women making policy and giving advice on major decisions? I know of very few, and that goes for all the candidates of both major parties. In short, nothing had changed, except that the techniques of merchandising candidates had been expanded to include spurious appeals to newly important blocs of voters. There was no real, primary concern for the rights and needs of blacks, of Indians, of women. Most of the Democratic candidates said most of the right things on issues affecting blacks, but it was done in the paternalistic, white-liberal style. Blacks were clients, recipients of benevolence, not full partners and equal fellow citizens. The candidates did not live what they talked about. It was the old hypocrisy, new model.

Since I went to the House of Representatives in 1969, I have grown to detest many of the white Northern liberals who are always ready with rhetoric about equal opportunity in jobs and education, and so on and so on. When the time comes to put the heat on, in committee and on the floor, and *do* something, like passing an amendment or increasing an appropriation, too many of these white knights turn up missing. They have urgent business elsewhere, even on the paddle-ball court of the House gymnasium (I do not exaggerate; key votes have been lost because members whose votes were being counted on were in the gym). They do just enough to preserve their images, to get by with passing grades. Give me a Southern conservative every time. I know who he is and where he's coming from. It's all out there in the open, and I can deal with him.

What I mean is that the "new" politicians have no more real concern about poor people than the older liberals, no true belief in the brotherhood of races, no understanding of how women are victimized and oppressed by prevailing attitudes and institutions. They appear to be concerned, but it is not genuine. If they were honest with themselves, they would realize that their actual interest in minorities is just as an instrument to help them retain political power.

New politics needs new men and women. Increasing participation in the process does not mean much if the new participants still have to make the same old choices, between one white "liberal" upper-middle-class, college-educated, well-off middle-aged male and another. It is time we had different options. There ought to be more nontraditional candidates. Everyone is barred now from seeking high office unless he fits the mold. Are all wisdom, all talent, all leadership, all intelligence, all ability, all creativity concentrated in this one group? If not—as it is obvious they are not—is not our society losing a great deal by its habitual pattern of delegating power: a few white men lead, everyone else follows? Could it be that the persistence of poverty, hunger, racism, war, semiliteracy and unemployment is partly due to the fact that we have excluded so many persons from the processes that make and carry out social policies?

As a black woman active in national politics, these

questions have long preoccupied me, and I do not need to say what I believe the answers to them are. But how do we change the way things are? What could *I* do to change them? This was the real question. It does no good to say, "Something ought to be done," or "Somebody ought to do something." Until you realize that the important question is "What am I going to do?" you have not begun to be serious about a problem. For this reason—and for a number of others—I began, during 1971, to think more and more about what seemed to very many persons to be a ridiculous idea. Suppose *I* were to run for President?

III.

The Kids

RUNNING FOR PRESIDENT was not my idea originally. It was a number of college students who started me thinking seriously about it, against what I first thought was my better judgment. It began as far back as 1969, my first year in Washington. Before the end of my second term in the House, I had spoken on well over one hundred campuses in forty-two states, and on most of them someone had asked me, "Why don't *you* run for President in 1972?"

Not many members of Congress fill as many college speaking dates as I do; for one thing, not many are asked to. Some of the liberal stars and a handful of ex-professors are exceptions. But most Congressmen go where the votes are, to events in their districts or, if they speak elsewhere, it is normally as a favor to another politician. No doubt I was originally sought because of my novelty value as the only black woman in Congress. But it soon became more than that, and the invitations flooded in—three times as many as I could handle—because something in me and an audience of students strikes a spark. There is a street slang word, jive, that comes to mind. Many people know it only as an out-of-date word for hot music. But what it really means is to tell lies and talk big to see if you can fool someone. No better characterization could be found of the style of a lot of officeholders, and the fact that they are jiving is instantly perceived by young audiences. Student groups don't always agree with the things I say; I speak at all kinds of colleges, North and South, black and white, and I never tailor what I say to the audience. But whatever they think of my ideas, they can tell that I'm not jiving, and that, I guess, is the explanation of why they respond to me.

What is it about them, on the other hand, that leads me frequently to turn down engagements that might be lucrative or politically advantageous to speak at a college instead? It is fairly simple: those kids keep my hope alive. I would get on a plane after a day of frustrating losses in a House committee or on the floor, after seeing a bill to start building a national system of day care centers, for instance, killed by the President with a callously phony excuse dreamed up by some right-winger, or after seeing an appropriation for murder in Vietnam sail through while one for more housing stays locked in committee. You wonder what is the use of coming back the next day; the majority of Congress clearly doesn't care about the children who don't have a clean, safe place to stay while their parents are at work, about the jobless men and women who have lost all hope of supporting themselves and their families except with welfare and food stamps, about . . . the list is endless. And the majority of the country doesn't care enough to throw these people out of office and replace them with representatives who would work for the victims of society instead of the victors. And what hope is there that it will ever be much different? Feeling that way, I go out and give one of my speeches. Afterward there is almost always a question period, and the questions always cover the standard litany of issues—war spending, poverty, health, housing, racism, unemployment. But what is different is that the students are really concerned about these things, puzzled and angry that more people are not as concerned, and determined to do something about them. When the great problems are so well known, why is no real action being taken on them? Why do so many men in office pay lip service to the need, but little more? Who is there on the political scene who offers a credible hope of changing the way things are? Often the discussion becomes so engrossing that the kids won't let it end; I plead that I have to get up early to catch a plane back to Washington, but they beg me to stay a little longer and pack me into a car to lead a procession to a coffee shop or dormitory lounge, where we go on talking until one or two o'clock in the morning.

When I go back to a motel, or to some faculty member's house where I am staying, I have had most of my frustration and despair washed away by contact with those kids. They really see what is wrong, even if their knowledge of the problems is more likely to be based on reading than on experience; they perceive that no one is seriously trying, for instance, to revitalize the decaying cities or provide decent medical care for millions who cannot afford it. They are angry that this is the way things are. The great thing about them is that they have not learned to take no for an answer. And, unlike many adults, neither have I. That is why they give me new hope, every time I talk with them.

Exactly where it happened, I am no longer sure, but it was at a Southern school. A young man asked me why I didn't run for President, and I gave him the answer I had been giving for three years, laughing as I said it: "You don't know what you're asking me to do. You must understand, whatever my ability to handle the job, and regardless of your belief in me, I am black and I am a woman." This young man—he was white, if that matters—would not accept that. "Well," he demanded, "when are we going to break this tradition? We've had a lot of speakers here, and none of them has dealt with the issues the way you have. We need somebody who will do that." And then he said, "Don't worry. We will be voting soon, and we will support you if you run."

What he said stayed with me for some reason. It was not his promise of support, sincere though it probably was, but that question, "When are we going to break this tradition?" When? Never, if we don't start now. The more I thought, the less I could see any other answer to his question. It was many months later that I finally decided to run, but looking back, I can see the germ of the decision began there.

It is really astonishing when one stops to recapitulate the last dozen years and realizes how many of the most important themes in politics have been sounded first by young people and gradually, painfully forced on reluctant elders. The beginning was the civil rights movement of the early 1960s, and if one needs a precise moment, it was at Greensboro, North Carolina, when a small group of black students staged the first of a series of sit-ins and desegregated a five-and-ten-cent store lunch counter. From that beginning blossomed the voter registration drives and other campaigns that drew college students—more white ones than black at first—into active politics. It was a romantic, radical, impetuous, youthful style of politics, but politics nevertheless. That era of "black and white together . . . we shall overcome" lasted until 1965 at the latest; it was already ending in 1964. The civil rights movement stalled and split in two, with white youth going one way, to wind up in anti-war activity, and black youth another way, many into the "black power" movement originated by Stokely Carmichael. But look what had been accomplished because the young activists had spurred the public conscience: the 1964 Civil Rights Act banned racial discrimination in hotels, restaurants and most other public places, and the 1965 Voting Rights Act wiped out literacy tests and other devices used to keep blacks off the voter rolls in the South. Neither would have been enacted if youthful activists had not (in the now-current phrase) raised the public's consciousness.

In a series of lectures on contemporary politics that I

have given at the New School and elsewhere I like to quote at this point Jack Newfield, the one-time activist with the Students for a Democratic Society and now a radical journalist and theoretician. He believes that the civil rights movement liberated more white middle-class students than it did Southern working-class Negroes. He means, as I interpret it, that it freed them of their fear of doing something different, something possibly dangerous, something to mark them out from the crowd. And I think he also means that it freed them of their assumption that everything in our society is on the whole going well, and getting better. Young whites learned to see America from a new angle, the viewpoint of its black victims. Once they did that, they began to question other things. Even before Vietnam became an important issue, they questioned the cold war and the arms race. (The famous peace symbol, it is often forgotten, originally came from the semaphore code for N–D, meaning nuclear disarmament.)

The young civil rights campaigners, black and white, acquired a feeling that not only were many things amiss, but that they could do something to change the conditions. Along with discontent, they found hope. For the white kids it was group psychotherapy on a massive scale; it lifted them out of their apathy and showed them how to transcend themselves.

No political history of the years from 1962 to 1972 can be a faithful one unless it pays close attention to the unprecedented fact that a new generation during those years decided, almost en masse, to lay hands on their society and change it. Most older people did not understand what was going on while it was happening, and still do not. Their heads are full of stereotypes of hairy, dope-smoking, foul-mouthed young anarchists. What they saw on television and read in most newspapers amounted only to the froth on the waves; the underlying facts were never reported. Take, for instance, the series of events at Cornell University in 1969, when the country was shocked to see black students carrying guns out of Willard Straight Hall, which they had been occupying for more than a day. Guns! An armed revolt on one of our old ivied campuses! The impact of those pictures still remains. The impression left by the media is that a group of blacks grabbed guns and took over the building, threatening to start shooting if their demands were not met.

The facts were quite different, and it is instructive to compare the whole story with what most people thought happened. To begin with, Cornell had recently admitted numbers of black students for the first time—not large numbers, but more than before. Black students had not been unheard of at Cornell earlier, but they were upper-middle-class blacks, dentists' and lawyers' and preachers' sons and daughters. But the newcomers were not all children of black professional parents, the kind of black that Cornell and other Ivy League schools had learned to live with. They were from working-class families, and their style was different. It aroused hostility. Murmured threats followed them around the campus, and angry stares met them downtown.

The black students, in turn, had many discontents. They felt a pardonable counter-hostility. They saw that they were not being given a fair chance to succeed, because so many of them came from substandard schools. They thought more black students should be admitted. They felt isolated and mistreated.

One night a cross was burned on the lawn of a house where a number of black women students lived. The black men reacted to that cross-burning, climaxing the mounting fear and frustration they had been feeling, with an angry and irrational move. That weekend was Parents' Weekend. They took over the student union building and drove out a number of parents who were housed there. Barricading it, they refused to leave until they got promises to put in motion what they saw as the solution to their problems.

It was many hours after the original occupation that firearms were passed in to them by students outside, and it was done because the students inside believed they were in danger of their lives. Perhaps they were wrong. But students had been shot down by police and National Guardsmen before, and would be again. They had been the targets of threats. And they well knew that in upstate New York nearly everyone is armed—it is a region of deer and small game hunters. Then there had been the burning of the cross. Given the history of the United States, I think any black citizen even today has reason to be frightened at a flaming cross.

What they did may have been poor judgment, and arming

themselves may have been wrong. But seen in perspective, it was not the senseless, violent action that it seemed to be in the television newsreels and most newspaper stories.

I tell this story at length to show that student rebellions are seldom, if ever, the irrational and anarchistic behavior that older people believe they are. Each one is comprehensible and many are praiseworthy, when we take the trouble to examine them. In the great Columbia revolt, the trouble was rooted in the university's callous attitude toward the black community that had grown up around it, and its deep involvement in war-making through Defense Department research and development work. Both were perceived by the students, and I think correctly, to be evils that needed to be ended. Later, the violent behavior of the police confirmed the students' alienation and rebellion.

The white middle-class student rebel was hard for his parents to understand at first because his goals seemed to them so strange. He had everything, they felt—a good home, money, clothes, an education, a career ahead. How could he say he was against a system that had given him so many things earlier generations struggled for and often did not win? This was the initial reaction, at least, in the 1960s. Some older persons are more sophisticated now and, at least as I write, the violent phase of student activism seems to be history. But to return to the question, one explanation was that today's younger people, having so many material things, have been free to look beyond them. It was not until man had secured his basic needs—shelter, food, safety from attack—that he developed the beginnings of the arts, that his religion began to grow from superstition into an ethical system, and that theoretical as well as practical learning began to take place. Students' involvement with social problems may be a new form of that familiar evolution. But the explanation does not entirely satisfy me.

Why does their discontent take such radical form? The word "radical," properly used, means going to the basis of a problem—the word comes from the Latin for "root"—rather than dealing with its manifestations. In common usage, radicals are distinguished from liberals by their willingness to question basic assumptions and work outside the system, while liberals work for change within the status quo. Most of today's youth are, in either sense, radical. In 1969, *Fortune* magazine made an extensive survey and concluded that about 750,000 of the country's 6,700,000 college students at that time "identified with the New Left," and that about 3,000,000 more shared many of its beliefs, especially in lacking a concern about making money. So widespread a phenomenon is not superficial or transitory, and could not be (as some Congressmen still believe) the work of a few agitators, of a small group of "hard-core militants and revolutionaries." The civil rights sit-ins, the voter registration drives, the agitation against the Southeast Asia war, and all the other campaigns led by younger citizens were each, in turn, written off as nothing but the work of a few "hard-core militants." Events proved the writers-off wrong in every case.

The generation I am speaking of, which is in its twenties and thirties now, was the first one to grow up and come of age in a world that appeared at every moment in real danger of annihilation. This is not a coincidence. The famous generation gap seems to me to be fairly clearly drawn between those who were children before 1945 and those who grew up after that. Some fundamental quality of life had changed; it was no longer possible to be sure there was a future. What does a young person believe in, growing up in such a world? He is likely to believe, on some deep, unverbalized level, that he has been betrayed—that his elders have given evidence that they are not fit to manage things. If we do not save the world, who will? That is their cry. The Berlin airlift, the Cuban crisis, the missile race, and finally Vietnam were the background of the childhood of the generation that is now around thirty. It was not that they understood and directly reacted to these events, but signs were in the air, and most of all they reacted to the reactions of older persons—families, teachers, television commentators.

Add to that foundation of deep insecurity the social troubles of the 1950s and 1960s, the racial problems thrust into public view (after centuries of near-invisibility) by minority migration into the big cities; economic dislocations caused by social changes, new technologies and an exploding population; and the effect of throwing open higher education to increasing numbers of middle- and lower-class students, who found themselves often at odds with the elitist traditions of the institutions they were attending, institutions designed for the upper classes and those who were trying to climb into them. There, I think, we have the background.

Then, in 1961, John F. Kennedy took office, and his energy, youthfulness and apparent idealism stirred younger Americans who had found little to admire in his predecessor. They began to believe in the possibility of action to improve the world they had inherited. Suddenly there were causes to fight for: civil rights, the underdeveloped countries (through the Peace Corps), university reform. Kennedy's murder was a deep shock, but at first Lyndon B. Johnson seemed to be carrying on. However, by 1965 or 1966, it began to be clear that something was wrong with the Great Society.

The Civil Rights Act had not produced equality: every one of its provisions was being flouted, in the South and in the North. The war in Vietnam was beginning to escalate; casualty lists began to appear. Television brought the bloodshed into every home, a new phenomenon which may have fed the anti-war revulsion. It became clearer that our society was not able to solve its problems at home while, insanely, it was trying to solve the world's problems and making them worse. Such immoral behavior was intolerable. The years 1965 and 1966 were years of teach-ins on hundreds of campuses. Their message of the immorality of the war was rejected at first, but slowly it began to be accepted by a growing number of Americans. The anti-war movement arrived at the center of the political arena in 1968, when it compelled Johnson to abdicate and created Eugene McCarthy to be its leader for a while. (McCarthy's banner, and part of his movement, fell into the hands of George McGovern four years later, but that is a different chapter in the story.)

Young radicals failed to capture the Democratic Party in 1968; the party's traditional liberals, who believe in social justice but are comfortable with the status quo, hung on and put up Hubert H. Humphrey, one of the best of their kind. Humphrey, campaigning, put his arm around Chicago Mayor Richard Daley, the author of the police riot during the 1968 convention, confirming the kids' belief that conventional politics is an absurdity.

After 1968 some young people turned off on politics; some took up apolitical causes like the environment; some decided to concentrate on local issues and candidates. They waited for 1972 to see if next time would be different. As 1972 came closer, they began to suspect strongly that it was not going to be. The same old faces came forward with the same old song-and-dance: Humphrey, Nixon, Muskie, Jackson and company. Some of the kids turned to McGovern; he seemed to be the best of the lot, the only possibility, so they pinned their faith on him. Others could not accept McGovern and looked for a new approach, a different angle of attack, some way to shake up the system and force it to realize it must change. The suggestion that I be a candidate came from young people like those, and they gave me my earliest and some of my most loyal support.

IV.
Black Politics

DURING THE EARLY part of 1971, black politicians and civic leaders began to think and talk about whether the time had come to run a black candidate for President in the 1972 election. The strengths and weaknesses of such a strategy were fairly clear from the start, and they seemed to balance each other so evenly that it was extremely difficult to reach a decision. The idea arose from deep discontent with the Democratic Party, which had taken the black vote for granted for years on the cynical but sound theory that blacks had nowhere else to go. Could a black candidate swing enough votes behind him to go to the Democratic National Convention with a solid bloc of delegates that would compel the powers in the party to listen to black demands? It was an exciting idea. Not just blacks, but other minorities, could negotiate for once from a position of strength if they had enough votes to deny the nomination to anyone except a candidate who would pledge himself to vigorous action on employment, day care, housing, education, equal employment rights, genuine welfare reform, health care and the other issues that concern minorities. But could a coalition of local and state leaders, from areas where the black vote is concentrated enough to make itself felt, be formed and held together for the twelve months it would take to arrive at the convention with the votes in hand? A bigger question was, could these delegates rally behind one candidate, submerging ideological and personal differences? And the biggest question of all, who could the candidate be?

Apart from these practical difficulties in carrying out the plan, there was good reason to doubt that it was a sound strategy. In the past, blacks and other minorities have invariably acted on the lesser-evil principle and supported the white candidate who seemed most liberal, most sympathetic and likeliest to give their needs at least a hearing. What would be lost if they succeeded in switching black votes to a black candidate, and away from an electable white candidate who represented the lesser evil, thereby causing the election of one who was a greater evil? Suppose, in crucial states like New York and Illinois, a black candidate won a handful of delegates and in doing so handed control of the state delegations to a Henry Jackson instead of a Hubert Humphrey? Where would the black strategy be then?

But the pitfalls did not seem important, compared to the prize to be won if the strategy succeeded—a genuine voice in national policy for minorities for the first time. Black leaders, so called and otherwise, began to telephone each other, talk of meetings, and finally to organize conferences. For the most part, I had very little to do with the debates; I was not asked to take much part, and I did not intrude. In September, 1971, the first activity surfaced. Leaders of the eastern regional conference of the Congress of African Peoples (a separatist group concentrated in Newark and led by Heywood Henry and Imamu Amiri Baraka) met and announced that state political conventions would be held to name black tickets in at least twelve states, and the congress would join in a National Black Political Convention that would decide how best to influence the 1972 Democratic National Convention.

About the same time, Representative John Conyers of Detroit popped up with a candidate, Mayor Carl Stokes of Cleveland. If Stokes were supported by all blacks, Conyers said, his candidacy would create a black caucus with increased bargaining power at the convention. Stokes' urban experience qualified him for the Presidency, but Conyers did not contend that Stokes really had a chance to be nominated.

Stokes, Conyers said, was the most eligible candidate, one who had already made a very important contribution to American politics (as he had in becoming the mayor of a major city). Stokes was popular, he said, well-known, able and "not running [for mayor] again." Conyers had not consulted with Stokes before his endorsement and had no indication that Stokes would run. "It is just something that I am doing on my own," the Michigan Congressman explained.

He said he did not believe a black candidate should run for a third or fourth party nomination—this would only dissipate potential black voting power—but running for the Democratic nomination could have considerable effect.

Stokes had been elected mayor of Cleveland in 1967 and reelected in 1969. In his first year in office in Cleveland, there was a shoot-out between police and black militants that left ten dead. It also left severe racial tensions that plagued Stokes' administration. Conyers was quite restrained in saying that Stokes was available because he was not running again. Few in Cleveland thought he would have a chance if he ran. His career as mayor had been marked by bitter battles with the City Council, and relations had deteriorated to such a point that in the spring of 1971 Stokes and his chief assistants boycotted council meetings. On April 16, he suddenly announced that he would not seek a third term, saying, "I have been privileged to serve in high office during America's most trying time, but my services have of necessity been limited to a very small constituency. I want now to expand my efforts." What he had in mind, it developed, was to organize a "people's lobby" to bring pressure on both major parties to choose responsive candidates for 1972. Stokes' response to Conyers' endorsement was that he was highly sympathetic to the idea of having minority groups win a greater voice in the selection of candidates by both major parties, but he did not want to be the standard-bearer. He mentioned five other black leaders as "deserving utmost consideration" for national office: Manhattan

Borough President Percy Sutton, Mayor Richard Hatcher of Gary, the Reverend Jesse Jackson (at the time head of Operation Breadbasket in Chicago), Conyers and me.

In July I had begun dropping hints that I might run in some primaries; this was partly a calculated move to see what the response would be and partly an honest expression of indecision. How could I think of running for President with no money to finance a campaign, and if I did raise the money by some miracle, would it all be wasted? How many people were there who desired change enough to support someone who was out to shake things up? There were many college students—fine, some of them would even go as far as to vote for me and some would work for me. There were women's groups who, like the students, had been urging me to run. There were ordinary black and white, Jewish, WASP, and Spanish-surnamed citizens here and there who kept telling me, "You're what this country needs." But I knew what I would be getting into. Into debt, for one thing. And I knew, as my would-be supporters did not, what a controversy my candidacy would stir up in the black community, between blacks and other groups, and within the Democratic Party. I talked about running, but I was very far from being resolved to run.

During September, 1971, something happened that gave new force to the move for a national black coalition. Senator Edmund S. Muskie, who most experts agreed was on his way to being the Democratic nominee, said he did not think the nation was ready to accept a black nominee for Vice

President, and at least by implication said that he would not consider a black running mate. Muskie said he thought the prevailing opinion was wrong, because America is a country where a black should be eligible for consideration as part of a national ticket. Some people thought Muskie was speaking with the candor that had made him so attractive in 1968. That may have been, but it was a major blunder, one of the first of many that drove Muskie out of the contest. Naturally, charges that his statement amounted to bigotry came from many sources in the black community. Such a charge was unfair, of course. But what mattered in the long run was that Muskie had all but assured he would not have the future support of black voters, which he might well have earned if he had not made such a statement, and if he had made a genuine effort to understand what blacks needed and pledged himself to action to obtain it.

One of the key events of late 1971 was the Northlake meeting, named for the section of greater Chicago, near O'Hare International Airport, where black politicians and civil rights leaders from several parts of the country met in a closed two-day meeting, within a tight ring of security. Its purpose was to chart a course for blacks in the 1972 election. But most of those arriving for the meeting refused to tell reporters why they had come. "This must be the biggest secret since the atomic bomb," Roy Innis, leader of the Congress of Racial Equality, joked to one reporter as he ducked into a hotel elevator. Innis' and Imamu Baraka's bodyguards kept outsiders from a spiral staircase leading to the meeting room. (I might remark that no elected black officials I know have bodyguards, only the self-appointed and media-anointed ones, and they must know better than I why it is they need them.)

Invitations to the meeting were sent out by Julian Bond, the handsome young Georgia state representative. Julian, Percy Sutton, Richard Hatcher and California state representative Willie Brown organized the affair. Each of them, and many of the other participants, had his own ideas. Dr. John Cashin, chairman of the Alabama National Democratic Party, wanted no part of a black Presidential candidate and had a resolution from a Southern Black Caucus meeting in August to back him up. In fact, the resolution went even further and urged blacks to stay aloof "from the entire list of candidates for the Presidency of the United States." Percy Sutton was of exactly the opposite opinion. He told a reporter, about the same time as the Northlake meeting, "Running a black Presidential candidate creates a strategy and a sense of internal unity which carries far beyond the convention floor and the election of 1972. It carries with it a political awareness that will flow into the local elections of every city, town and village in America where black people live."

Several of the participants circulated position papers. One was Bond, who urged that each state or city with a good-sized black population run a well-known black as a favorite son or daughter candidate (the "daughter" was a nod to me) in the primaries. Local leaders would have a better effect in getting out the black vote than a national figure, and besides, where was there a potential candidate of the stature required? As Bond's scenario went, the favorite sons (and daughters) would each bring a pocketful of delegates to the Democratic convention and meet to combine them.

For some participants, the stress was not on deciding on a black candidate, or candidates, but on planning some way to maximize the effect blacks would have on the platform and programs of the Democratic Party. One of the papers that circulated at Northlake gave the sixty recommendations sent to President Nixon by the Congressional Black Caucus early in 1971, and urged that black support be extended or denied to candidates on the basis of their positions on the Black Caucus platform. At that point, Senator George McGovern was the only candidate who had endorsed the whole list and he, it developed later, had a couple of reservations.

The cast of black figures at the meeting was to become a familiar one in the ensuing months: Baraka, Bond, Innis, Jesse Jackson, Sutton, Hatcher, Clarence Mitchell III (a Maryland state senator) and Basil Patterson, who had been an unsuccessful candidate for lieutenant governor of New York. Meeting after meeting would be held, each with the same outcome—no plan, no unity and nothing agreed on except to hold more meetings. Foreseeing this, and because I divined that if I attended I would be the focus of much of the dissension, I stayed away from Northlake and the succeeding conclaves, but I sent my chief political operative, Thaddeus Garrett. Others who were invited but did not attend were Conyers, Stokes and the Reverend Ralph D. Abernathy of the Southern Christian Leadership Conference.

Reporters, barred from the meeting, clustered outside and extracted what they could from the participants who were willing to talk to them. The resultant mystery made the meeting sound a lot more significant in the newspapers than it really was.

Inside, there was already being heard an argument against my candidacy that would be raised again and again: Shirley Chisholm would not be a candidate who was for blacks, she would be the candidate of women. Thadd Garrett both argued in the meeting and told reporters later about it, saying, "When a black politician asks if she would be the candidate of blacks or the candidate of women, and what would happen when the deal goes down and something has to be bargained away, I tell him, 'She is a black woman, of the black experience, and from one of the blackest districts in the country. She can do nothing but be black in her dealings.' " What was really bothering the black males at the meeting was more directly hinted at by one who told a Washington *Post* reporter (anonymously—I don't know who he was), "In this first serious effort of blacks for high political office, it would be better if it were a man." It was what I would later come to define as "the woman thing"; if anyone thinks white men are sexists, let them check out black men sometime. Representative Ronald Dellums of

California, one of the few in high places who understood what I was doing from the start and supported me almost all the way, was also one of the few who were able to transcend those feelings. He told the same Washington *Post* man, "She could have a dramatic effect on politics in this country. She could bring together the elements necessary to create a third force in American politics, and by 1976 we would be able to put together a ticket that would win."

The black coalition eluded the grasp of the participants in the Northlake meeting, as it was to do repeatedly in the next ten months. But there was a unity of feeling, despite the dissension over methods, that kept drawing them together again and again.

Something happened to me in October that was of no great importance to anyone else but stands out in my memory and played a part, I think, in my decision to run. In Chicago, the Reverend Jesse Jackson and his Operation Breadbasket held a Black Expo, the third annual Chicago exhibit of black achievements in business, cooperative projects, the arts and other fields. I was to speak, along with Coretta King, at a workshop on women in politics. As I went into the convention hall, three or four black men came in at the same time. They were middle-aged and conservatively dressed; I took them for politicians. They saw me, and one of them said to the others, loud enough for me to hear, "There she is—that little black matriarch who goes around messing things up." I was furious, but all I did was wheel around and give them a hard stare. As I went on into the hall, I knew suddenly what I was going to say at the workshop. Women in politics? Women were intruders in politics in the eyes of men like these, and most black men were like these. When were they going to get off our backs?

"Black women," I said when my turn came, "have got to realize what they are in for when they venture into politics. They must be sure they have the stamina to endure the endless obstructions that are put in their way. They must have enough self-confidence so they will not be worn down by the sexist attacks that they will encounter on top of racial slurs." I repeated what I have said many times, that during twenty years in local ward politics, four as a state legislator and four as a member of Congress, I had met far more discrimination because I am a woman than because I am black. Carried away a little, I went on:

"You have heard that I am considering running for President, and you may wonder how I have the nerve to say such a thing when I know that the sexist opposition I have had in the past, on top of the racial prejudice I have faced, will seem like nothing compared to what I can expect to have if I do run. Well, I am about ready to make my decision to run, and I just want today to say a few things to my black brothers, who I know are not going to endorse me. I do not expect their support, nor will I bother them about it. I know their feelings. I have learned too much for too long in my dealings with politicians, black and white. There are people who believe I should go to these men and discuss my intentions with them, but this kind of thinking is folly.

Anyone in his right mind knows that this group of men, for the most part, would only laugh at the idea. They would never endorse me. They are the prisoners of their traditional attitudes, and some of them are just plain jealous, because they have been wounded in their male egos. They will deny this, of course, but their denials are only another aspect of the male vanity at work."

When I arrived at the convention hall, I had no intention of making such a strong statement. But that remark I heard as I entered was one I had heard just once too often. There comes a time when the heart is full and one is sick of keeping quiet out of a sense of the need for unity. If you store these things up inside for too long, in the end you become ill under the strain. I had no intention of doing that any longer, and I let it all out. I decided it was time for my brothers to know where I was coming from and what I was about to do.

"Get off my back!" I said, and that was the line all the newspapers in Chicago used the next day. "If I make the race, I want it to be clear that it will be without seeking anyone's endorsement. The endorsements I have so far have come from those who are not regarded as leaders, men who play a role in the decision of who will run for President. My backing is coming from just plain people, and that is enough for me. That will be my inspiration, if I do make the decision to accept the challenge, and see whether I can be a catalyst for change in this country, an instrument the people can use to shake up the system."

In the last few months, I said, I had caught hell because

I publicly supported freedom on bail for Angela Davis, who was then awaiting trial (in which she was ultimately acquitted of a murder charge). I had gone to my brothers in Congress and in leadership positions elsewhere and asked them to join me, and they told me they could not because it was not politically expedient for them. And now these same men were criticizing me publicly and privately on the grounds that they doubted my commitment to black causes; they hinted that I would sell out black interests if they came in conflict with those of women. *They* were questioning *my* commitment. It was incredible. But I did not dwell on that any longer.

"Brothers," I concluded, "black women are not here to compete or fight with you. If we have hang-ups about being male or female, we're going to waste the talents that should be put to use to liberate our people. Black women must be able to give what they have in the struggle."

Women came up to me to tell me they felt the way I did but had never dared to say so in public. They told me how they had been insulted by both black and white men in local and county civic organizations. If I ran for President, they said, they were sorry for me because of the humiliations I would have to face. "I can handle them," I said. "That's been the story of my life."

The outburst made me feel better and put me fairly on the record as to what my relationship to the self-appointed leaders of the problematic black coalition would be. One other thing it accomplished was to lay partly to rest a theory that I was acting only as a stalking-horse for New York Mayor John V. Lindsay. Based on the close and friendly relations Lindsay and I had maintained since 1970, when I was one of the few black office-holders in New York City to endorse him early in his reelection campaign, such stalking-horse rumors had circulated at the Northlake meeting. My absence from the gathering seemed, apparently, to give them credibility. One newspaper writer, columnist William N. Banks, Jr., of the weekly *Manhattan Tribune,* in a postmortem on Northlake that appeared a few days after my speech at Black Expo, said it seemed that there was no foundation for believing that I was really aiding Lindsay. But Banks thought I should have gone to Northlake; my absence "did not help to clarify the confusion."

A lot of people felt that way, who did not see the political situation the way I did during the fall of 1971. First, I believed that if a black coalition were to be formed, it would not be done by some of the gentlemen who were organizing the meetings. Second, I understood that if the coalition did somehow take shape, there was no realistic possibility that it would endorse me. This was the situation: everyone was talking about the need to form a black bloc at the national convention. It was clear from the start (clearer than it was to seem as the convention got closer) that any endorsement of a white candidate, given the choices of white candidates available, would look like a sellout to black voters. But the black coalition's would-be leaders had an insuperable problem. There were too many generals and too few soldiers.

The more they tried to arrive at a strategy for 1972, the more alienated they became from each other, because of the philosophical and ideological differences among them. The social revolution taking place in the country had placed blacks in many camps—integrationists, separatists, moderates, militant extremists—all with different points of view on how to organize and for what goal, and all vying for broader support among the black masses. They seemed to think that their common skin pigmentation would somehow produce a magic sympathy and agreement, and that if they met enough and talked enough, the rhetoric would eventually culminate in a plan that, even if not totally acceptable, would unite them for action. But there was no chance of this unless there could be found a way to submerge the underlying differences among the various black leaders, elected, appointed or self-appointed.

A moving figure in all these black meetings was Imamu Amiri Baraka, the poet, playwright and nationalist leader. Imamu is a separatist who, to be consistent, should work outside the existing political structure, but who is intelligent enough to know that that would make him unacceptable to the broad majority of blacks. It is inevitable that, when he engages in electoral politics, his promises collide with those of blacks who are committed to the election process. He tries to bridge the gap with a slogan: "Unanimity without Uniformity." But in the real political world his slogan does not work. To unite, some differences have to be laid aside. If blacks are to become a force in the American political system, they will have to learn to relinquish personal ambition if it conflicts with the greater goals of black action. It will not be possible to insist on each detail of some radical program—or conservative program either, for that matter—as the price of cooperation. In the spring the same Northlake crowd was to hold a National Black Political Convention in Gary, Indiana. Again, Imamu Baraka would be a leading participant. He had a program he wanted adopted. Some of its elements were unacceptable to other black leaders—not only to me but to most or all of the Congressional Black Caucus, and to local officials like New York's Percy Sutton. Action on the convention "platform" was delayed and delayed while sessions were held devoted to one speech after another. Late on the last day, after more than half the delegates had wearied of the unprofitable goings-on and left, resolutions backing the Arab nations against Israel and condemning busing to desegregate school systems were shoved through by Baraka and his allies. It was uniformity without unanimity.

Although Baraka has been active in supporting Kenneth Gibson for mayor of Newark, and made forays into national politics, he has for some reason never submitted himself to the test of running for office. This is strange, because he could be a compelling candidate. The influence he wields at black political gatherings is almost entirely due to his personal qualities, his intelligence and his quiet but moving, persuasive speech, which many black elected officials cannot match. In a lot of ways, he fills a vacuum of leadership at these meetings, a fact that can perturb participants who think they have a better claim to lead than he. For my part, my only difficulty with Imamu is that I cannot understand how someone who holds such strong separatist views keeps trying to associate himself with those of us who still believe that, in spite of the inequities and grievances that persist, America can become a just, democratic, multifaceted society.

Most members of the Congressional Black Caucus attended one or another of the series of meetings, but only three were active and fairly regular participants—William Clay of Missouri, John Conyers of Detroit, and the Reverend Walter Fauntroy, the District of Columbia's nonvoting delegate in the House. Some of my friends and advisers thought I should have taken a part in the black meetings, but I was sure it was better to go my own way. Had I gone to any of them, I would have been the focus for all of the frustrations that they resulted in; I would have been the scapegoat for their inability to agree on a program. Evidence that I was right was not long in appearing. The word began to circulate, as it had earlier, that I was "on an ego trip," that I was really the women's candidate and didn't care about my people, that I was a stalking-horse for Lindsay, a stalking-horse for McGovern, a stalking-horse for Humphrey. My candidacy, some of the male leaders complained, was splitting the black bloc.

One thing that very few of the participants in these meetings saw, although some did, was that I was not out to become only the black candidate. While I would have welcomed the support of these men, I did not seek it because, even if they had offered me their backing (as I knew they never would do), I would have been locked into a false and limiting role. It was possible for me to be more than the black candidate, or the candidate of minorities generally. My potential support went far beyond the black community. It could come from the women's movement, from young voters, and even from a growing number of older white voters who had reached the end of their patience with the programs and candidates of the two major parties. Whether I could put together a coalition drawn from all these sources was doubtful, but who was there among the other candidates available to the embryonic black coalition who had that potential? In that sense, I was far and away the strongest black candidate because, paradoxically, I was not solely a black candidate. Had the black leaders decided that this was true, and united behind me by early 1972, I believe that I would have drawn as much as 85 percent of the black vote. But that was a fantasy then and later. They would never get *behind* me. Behind a woman? Unthinkable!

Julian Bond's "favorite-son" strategy, which he advocated at Northlake and for some time after, deserves attention by itself, because it was a subtle and attractive idea. Strong black candidates in Southern states like Florida, North Carolina and Tennessee, people well known to the voters there, could perhaps sell them the idea of electing a slate of black convention delegates which the local black leaders would take to the convention in the time-honored style of white politicians who want to keep their states' votes in line until they have struck the best bargain for delivering them. While there was no chance of carrying a whole state, realistically, the new party rules made it entirely possible that significant numbers of delegate contests could be decided by black voters. In the North, in pockets of black strength—Brooklyn, Harlem, Philadelphia, Washington, D.C., Chicago, Detroit, Los Angeles and elsewhere—local leaders could do the same thing. Bond's plan was based, it is clear, on his judgment that there was no potential black candidate of national stature. But there was Chisholm in Brooklyn, Jesse Jackson and others in Chicago, Dr. Aaron Henry and Charles Evers in Mississippi, and so on.

Bond's plan was, technically, a proposal to violate one of the McGovern Commission's party reform guidelines, which outlawed favorite-son candidacies. Certainly he knew this, and presumably he decided that there was nothing so sacred about the new guideline that it could not be flouted for the sake of a higher principle. Bond also saw a more cogent objection to his plan, that black candidates would cut into the vote of the more liberal white candidates and enhance the chances of more conservative or establishment candidates carrying the states where blacks were strongest. But he and his adherents felt the risk was justified by the trading power that blacks could take to the convention. Besides, he may have felt as I do, and as I know many blacks and other minorities feel. There isn't any difference between white conservatives and white liberals that makes much difference to us; the main thing we can see is that one talks a better game.

There was an enormous question that it seemed Bond did not face, or perhaps he begged it. Would all the local black favorite sons stay un-bought-off all the way to the convention? Events later in the campaign showed how unlikely this would have been. Another problem, perhaps as large, was that of whom they would unite behind and who would take the lead in speaking for the coalition in Miami. If they could not agree among themselves, at leisure, months before the convention, how could they function as a unit under the pressure, tension and haste of a convention? Bond made one more assumption that was shaky; it was clear he believed that the black vote would go in the end to someone like Hubert Humphrey, George McGovern or John Lindsay, after having been coyly withheld until McGovern or Humphrey or whoever came across with commitments to black and minority needs. But this left out of account that the black leaders each came from different sections of the country and had to go back home and live there after the convention. They had to deal, back home, with the Richard Daleys or the James Eastlands—a fact of life, and nobody ever got far in big-time politics by ignoring the facts of life. Many strong and effective local black leaders wanted no part in alienating the powers in the political structure. One such was Representative Augustus Hawkins of Watts, who was against the independent black bloc idea all the way. "Running a black candidate," Gus said at one point, "and just raising hell at the convention risks irritating other groups we need to join with." His view was one I did not share, but I could appreciate why he preferred to keep his lines intact to the party organization, the backers of white candidates, the unions and other interest groups, rather than sacrifice these relationships to the highly questionable goal of developing an independent black bloc.

It seemed to the men at Northlake, as it seemed to me, that this kind of politics had been tried over and over again and that black and minority interests had always suffered in the end. It was time to declare our independence from our one-time white liberal allies and try to forge the black vote into a cohesive unit. But a majority of those of us who were wrestling with the problem did not agree with Bond's plan. In my mind, it came down to an old political adage: "You can't beat somebody with nobody." Running favorite sons or, as some were urging, running uncommitted black delegate slates would not have enough appeal to get out the black voters, who are historically always recalcitrant at turning out to choose between alternatives that make no difference to them, as they see it.

Had the meetings at Northlake and elsewhere produced a potential nominee whom I could have supported, and whom I could have seen as an effective leader in creating the national black voting bloc, I would have abandoned my campaign and worked for him as hard as I worked for myself. But no one was put forward who—to be completely candid—compared with me as a potential vote-getter. Who among the others mentioned was already under real pressure to run? Who else already had volunteers begging to be allowed to set up state and local campaign organizations? For whom else was there grass-roots support among women, Spanish-speaking voters and college-age voters? The fact is that there was a vacuum into which I was propelled. This may have left, as someone told a newspaper reporter, "male egos bleeding all over the floor," but it seemed to me that there were more important issues involved than hemophilia of the masculine psyche. There was the role that a serious black candidate could play in the campaign, above and beyond the effort to piece together a significant bloc of black delegates. This would be to harass the "major candidates" on the issues.

"When a Shirley Chisholm stands up and talks about redistribution of income," Carl Stokes said later in the year, "about seeing that the poor get a minimum maintenance allowance of $5,500, then McGovern and Muskie and the others are going to have to either move over to the policy or declare themselves otherwise." Representative Charles Rangel of Harlem said, "We are going to force the candidates to declare themselves. Now the Democratic candidates try to walk in the middle of the road, to get the Southern as well as the liberal vote. Well, that's prostituting yourself, and we aren't going to tolerate it." This was the real opportunity for a black and minority candidate. All the jockeying to create a black delegate bloc large enough to be a force at the convention would turn out to be academic if—as finally happened, although it looked impossible toward the end of 1971—one of the white candidates emerged from the primaries with a commanding lead over the others. But the telling blows could be struck during the campaign. Candidates will make commitments then that they would disdain after they have the nomination locked up. They can be forced to declare themselves on the issues. Hungry for support, they are flexible and ready to deal. They are on the spot. Reporters ask, "Mr. Humphrey, the black coalition says there should be blacks and other minorities in top cabinet positions. [For all I know, he may have been asked this question, but I am just making it up as an example.] In your administration, would you appoint a black Secretary of Health, Education and Welfare, or a Spanish-surnamed Secretary of Housing and Urban Development, and if so, who?" This is getting down to cases, and the "major candidates" will rarely be compelled to get specific in that way unless someone is putting pressure on them by persistently raising the issues. They will talk instead about equal educational opportunities. "But, sir, does that mean you are for busing school children to end the segregation here in the Detroit school system?" At that point the candidate is forced to get serious. If he keeps on jiving, it will show. This would be the main function of my candidacy, to the extent that I was able to exercise it, I reasoned.

V

Making Up My Mind

Now it was early in December, 1971. Eleven months before the Presidential election. The white Senators were falling over each other, jostling for position in the gauntlet of primaries they were to run, from New Hampshire and Florida in March to California in June. Not one of them had involved women, minorities, poor people or noncollege youth in any meaningful way as they drew their campaign plans. They had their operatives to line up the black vote, all right. They were looking for people to put in the show window as "minority coordinators" or "women's department coordinators" or "youth coordinators." But these activities were, and were to remain, sideshows. The women, the young people, blacks, Chicanos, Indians—where were they when it came time to make policy, take stands on issues, plan strategy? They were not invited into the inner circles. McGovern's campaign organization was a cut above the others in this respect. One woman, Anne Wexler of Connecticut, a leader in that state's McCarthy campaign in 1967–68, was in the McGovern inner circle and stayed there, if some reports are true, despite efforts by other staffers to shunt her out. The McGovern organization was conspicuously young, it is true, but they were nearly all white, middle-class, college-trained, new-politics-liberal youths. As the campaign progressed, the bad effects of this were plain. Insulated by arrogance, they were convinced that they knew what minorities, women and other groups needed. Why bring them in? Humphrey and his group of veteran advisers, Lindsay and his City Hall gang and the rest were just as bad.

The women's movement, the infant black coalition and the related movements were struggling to make their presence felt. But they were splintered and in disarray. McGovern appealed to some, but he had no chance for the nomination. Muskie was far out in front, but what did he have to offer? Humphrey's credentials as a civil rights supporter were undeniable, but otherwise he was, in a phrase McGovern was to use, "a man of the past." In such a dilemma (or hexi- or hepti-lemma) it was natural that my candidacy began to gain appeal for a certain number of people. Clearly, I had to make up my mind whether I was in or out, by early January at the latest.

If I did decide to run, I could serve to give a voice to the people the major candidates were ignoring as usual. Although I could not win, I still might help all the people who were offering me support, by increasing their influence on the decision about who would be the Democratic nominee.

That did not seem an impossible goal; difficult, but not impossible. But practical questions had to be answered. Where could I hope to get the money to run even a limited campaign? Where should I concentrate my few resources to get the maximum effect? These were hard questions. My only experience in campaigning was on the Congressional District level. In Brooklyn I could make up by sheer effort for the fact that I had little money to run a campaign. In my first run for Congress, I had beaten a better-known and well-financed Republican candidate, James Farmer, by personal contact and sustained effort. Translating that approach into a campaign for national office was obviously ridiculous. But what else could I do? A media campaign was not even worth considering; there was no way I would ever raise the millions that it would take. I had no idea what a bare-minimum campaign would cost—filing fees, buttons and bumper stickers, postage, plane tickets, motels. It seemed to me that a quarter of a million dollars was the rock-bottom amount I needed. If I had that amount in hand by early January, I resolved, I would go ahead. If not, forget it. We would just wait and see whether all the people urging me to run were serious enough about it to come through with a few dollars apiece to make it possible. So we waited. A dollar trickled in here, another there. The trickle did not grow. Eventually, I realized I was being naïve. My husband, Conrad, and my political adviser, Wesley McD. Holder, had told me I couldn't raise significant amounts of money until I made an announcement and committed myself to run. I had to admit they were right. After I made a formal announcement a month later, committees began to spring up and hold fund-raisers. Checks and cash, almost all for less than ten dollars, began to arrive in the mail at my campaign offices in Brooklyn and Washington. In the end they added up to less than $95,000, while the campaign cost close to $300,000. My original quarter-million estimate was not far off.

If I had had the money to pay professionals to raise more funds, and other professionals to see that they were wisely spent, my campaign could have been a great deal more successful, and I would not have been left with a dismaying burden of debt that would have to be paid off out of my personal income, augmented by a stepped-up schedule of lecture appearances. Looking back, maybe I went about it the wrong way. But if I had tried to do it differently, I would probably never have run. The decision I made was to leave fund-raising and spending to local groups in each state and city. They would be responsible for everything. Whatever I could raise nationally would go for my own travel expenses and for the operation of a campaign office, which would have to be staffed entirely by volunteers. We would print position papers, pamphlets and promotional material, but not enough to supply everyone free. Instead, the material would go out as samples that the local organizations could duplicate at their own expense. Meanwhile I would operate on my American Express card.

Events would prove it to be an unsatisfactory solution to the money problem. It exposed my supporters to hustlers, for one thing. Later on in California, I was horrified to learn that there had been four or five fund-raising events which took in thousands of dollars—how many we never knew—from which not one cent ever reached the campaign organization. We tried to trace the hustlers who put them on, but they had disappeared, like the money. A strong national campaign organization might have prevented it. Another pitfall we did not foresee was that after the campaign the local and state organizations would fold up without paying some of their bills. Unable to find anyone responsible, the creditors sent the bills on to me. Week after week, during the summer and fall of 1972, they would keep coming in. Totally without resources, I had to try to raise the money by lecture tours. When they would be paid off, there was no way to guess.

If my case were unique, I would not dwell on it. But the sad thing is that it is typical. Everywhere in this country there are men and women who have real ability and new solutions to offer, but they will never have a chance to serve in public office because they do not have the money to run and win. Meanwhile, candidates who are wealthy to start with, or who are not scrupulous about where they get their financial support, run well-financed campaigns that land them in office—where they become, with a few exceptions, exactly the men and women whom we ought *not* to have representing us. Books have been written on this subject, but nothing is being done about it, and nothing will be until the public realizes that it is in the public interest to forbid all use of private money, personal or contributed, in campaigns for office. If campaigns were shorter, tightly regulated and financed entirely by public funds, a great stride toward real democracy would be taken.

The stress that lack of money forced me to put on local financing played a large part in dictating what primaries I would enter; to a large extent, and quite naturally, the support would be in the same places where I had the best chances of winning delegates, so it worked out fairly well. Sitting down to decide where to run, if I was to run, and getting what advice I could, mostly from people as inexperienced as I was in planning a national campaign, I came to a few clear conclusions. I would have to enter Florida, one of the two earliest primaries. On the same date, March 14, would be the New Hampshire primary, but it looked pointless to tramp through the snow when it appeared that Muskie had the state in his pocket and the rest of the votes would be split six ways from Sunday. Like many predictions in 1972, that one turned out to be wrong, but as far as my candidacy went, I probably reached the right decision. It was impossible, furthermore, to hope to campaign in both states on my shoestring budget. So New Hampshire was out, but Florida had to be in. If I did not enter there, it would create an indelible impression that I was not seriously in the running. Besides, the women's movement was strong in Florida; the state had a sizable black minority; and most of all, college students at campuses where I had spoken were urging me to enter and promising to work for me. Florida was a must. What else?

We looked at the states. Alabama: the New Democratic Party there could win delegates, and we had some contacts with them. Their strategy would be to challenge the regular Democrats as an uncommitted slate; I could not campaign in Alabama and interfere with this local decision, but if their delegates were seated in a credentials contest, I would have reason to hope for some votes. Colorado: McCarthy had been strong there in 1968; the Democratic Party is a reform-minded minority; we should look for support but probably not campaign actively. Georgia: an Atlanta woman, Barbara Geddes, had been advocating my candidacy and was ready to go to work as soon as I said the word. The state's delegates were chosen by a convention system, and the efforts Barbara led were to gain me six—the first delegates I won. Alaska, Arizona: nothing there for us. Iowa: it too has a convention system, and did not look promising. But to my surprise there was tremendous pressure from Iowa for me to run there. The precinct caucuses were to be in January, the earliest in the country, and I could not get away to campaign. But a Des Moines woman, Roxanne Conlon, and other supporters decided to see what they could do, and with less than three weeks to campaign, they got approximately 3 percent of the vote—not enough to win delegates, but a remarkable showing.

What about California? No, to win anything in

California I would have to carry the whole state with a plurality; it was one of eight remaining winner-take-all states, clinging to an old unfair system that the McGovern Commission had decided must be abolished. In California, we would just try to do some fund-raising; there was no point in spending time and energy there. Like several other decisions I made, this one would prove impossible to hold to. It was illogical to go into California, as I finally did, but there was nothing particularly logical about my campaign. In the end, I went in because so many Californians would not have it any other way, and as it turned out, I was glad I did.

So it went. We tried to be rational and orderly about it, but decisions about where to go and what to do were almost always made on a spur-of-the-moment, last-minute basis. It was a hell of a way to run a railroad, but it was the only way we had.

While all this planning and pondering was going on, I had a call from one of my colleagues, the Reverend Walter Fauntroy. Washington is the only major city with a black majority; it is nearly three-quarters black. It has a Presidential primary, and it promised to be one place I could be sure of getting some delegates. Mr. Fauntroy came to ask me not to enter. He knew that some people in the District, including political opponents of his—Julius Hobson, the Reverend Douglas Moore, the Reverend Channing Phillips—were after me to enter. They thought it would be significant if the District delegation at Miami were behind me. Fauntroy, maneuvering to become a nationally known black leader and simultaneously to strengthen his political hold on the District Democratic organization, had in mind to run as a favorite son. He did not know whether he could beat me on his home court or not. The betting was that we would split the thirteen delegates, with from five to eight of them going to me. The role Fauntroy had cast himself in for the Democratic National Convention would have been jeopardized if he did not go as the favorite son from the District of Columbia, with his bloc of votes to bargain with. He did not put the problem to me quite that way; he told me he thought it would be best for both of us not to be involved in a contest and that the main thing was to take the delegation to Miami as part of the convention black caucus. As the clincher, he promised to release the delegates to me on the second ballot. It was a hard decision to make; I did not want to aggravate tension in the Congressional Black Caucus, which would be certain to split on the question, with some supporting Fauntroy and some me, and others probably on the fence deploring the whole thing. But I did want those delegates. The important thing was to keep them uncommitted so they could be part of the black bloc at the convention. Fauntroy assured me that this was his sole intention. Later on, I would remember that assurance with a grim smile. Probably I made the right decision when I determined to stay out; going into the District primary would have had a divisive effect on the Congressional Black Caucus and could have sharpened divisions in the District party. My candidacy was already enough of a bone of contention among black leaders.

It was not that I hoped for the support of the caucus. Ron Dellums was already behind me, and Representative Parren Mitchell of Baltimore would endorse and campaign for me later on, but it had been clear that the caucus as a unit would not back me, at least as early as the late November meeting of black elected officials held in Washington, and sponsored by the caucus. Representative Louis Stokes was chairman of the arrangements, and the way the meeting was organized left me convinced that he, Representative William Clay of Missouri and other caucus members were out to do what they could to play down my candidacy. The point of the meeting was to bring the growing number of black officials, local, state and federal, together to talk about common problems and goals; it was not to work out a strategy for the Presidential election. But, naturally, everybody was talking about Presidential politics, and the fact was inescapable that I was the only black candidate moving at the time. The caucus asked its members to choose what workshops they would like to take part in during the meeting and I, because of my background as an educator and my position on the House Education and Labor Committee, asked to be included in a workshop on early childhood education. When the meeting got under way, it developed that there was also a workshop on national politics, and that I had not been included in the panel. State representative Gwendolyn Cherry of Miami, one of my earliest supporters, stood up to ask how it was that I had been left out, and a ruckus appeared to be developing. I raised my hand and was recognized. The reason I wasn't included was that no one had asked me, or even told me there was to be such a session, I said; I had picked the early childhood education workshop because of my interest in the field and because it is a question of major importance to black people; but if I had seen a complete list of the workshop topics that we had to choose from, naturally I would have picked national politics. It seemed to me clear that there had been a subtle but unmistakable attempt to keep me out of the limelight and that there was no possibility that I would ever gain the unified backing of the caucus.

At Gwen Cherry's invitation, I went to Miami for the Orange Bowl weekend in mid-December. The one thing on my mind was money; I spent the whole time talking to people about raising a campaign fund. The newspaper publicity was flattering and the promises of support I got were encouraging. I began to feel a little more confident that if I took the plunge the funds would follow; it is an illusion that a prospective candidate can easily acquire. By Christmas, I was resolved. I would leave for Florida to start campaigning right after New Year's, and I would make a formal announcement before the end of January.

VI

Florida

Just before Christmas, 1971, I got a note from Mayor John V. Lindsay, inviting me to Gracie Mansion. It said he had "something for me." I assumed it was a Christmas present. He and his wife greeted me and John and I sat down to talk. Behind the conversation I sensed an uncharacteristic tenseness, and I knew what it was. He wanted to find out whether I was determined to enter the Florida primary.

Two years earlier Lindsay had been reelected, against the odds, after his own party rejected him in the primary. He had switched to the Democratic Party and was looking for a way to rescue his career, once so promising, which had run into a dead end. There was hardly anyone who believed he could be reelected mayor of New York if he ran again; he could not aim at the Senate, because there was no way he could beat Jacob K. Javits and the other seat, held by conservative James L. Buckley, who might be vulnerable, would not be up for grabs until 1976. There were only two roads out for Lindsay and the crew of ambitious men around him: through the governor's mansion at Albany or through the primaries to the Democratic nomination. Lindsay had some reason to think he had as good a chance at the nomination as anyone, assuming Muskie left the race. He was telegenic, liberal and well financed. But the Florida primary would make or break him. Almost as soon as I started to drop hints that I was running, I began to get echoes from people in New York City that Lindsay was upset about it. He felt I could hurt him in Florida; he didn't care about other states, but Florida was crucial to him, and the black vote there—about 16 percent of the electorate—was vital. We met from time to time at functions, but he never mentioned my campaign. Clearly, that was what he wanted to talk about, but for some reason he was reticent. Finally I brought it up.

"Pressures are forcing me to make a decision to run," I said. "I know I don't have the resources, but the country is in such confusion, John, that I am being compelled to run as an alternative."

"You're going into Florida," he said.

"If I am serious, I have to show it by entering some primaries. Florida has blacks, youth and a strong women's movement, even though it is a Southern state, and those are some of the elements I hope I can appeal to. It is conceivable that I could do well in Florida."

Lindsay did not betray any emotion. After a pause, he asked me directly, "Do you have to go into Florida?"

"If I make my announcement in January, it's a foregone

conclusion," I said. "I will enter there. If I announce, Florida is the first place I'm off to." Lindsay said nothing more about it. We had never discussed it before, and we have not discussed it since. He gave me a beautiful painting—a city scene—and I thanked him.

During Lindsay's first campaign for reelection, when he was running as an independent, I was one of the few black leaders in New York City to endorse him early. Democrats criticized me for it and even said I ought to resign as a national committeewoman because I was not supporting the party's nominee. But there was no choice between Lindsay and the two conservatives the Republicans and Democrats were running; as a responsible leader in the black community, I had to say publicly that Lindsay was the only candidate of the three who deserved black support. When he won, he was naturally grateful; he formed the habit of keeping in touch with me and involving me in decisions, especially when they affected the black or Puerto Rican communities in Brooklyn. I got many a phone call from City Hall that began, "The mayor asked me to call you and see how you feel about . . ." There have been fewer since the Florida campaign.

John Lindsay and I were two of the darker horses in the Florida primary, which had just been moved back to March 14, making it one of the two earliest. The other, New Hampshire, seemed clearly pointless for me to enter, as I mentioned earlier. As a memo from one of my original campaign staff members, Virginia Kerr, put it: "New Hampshire is already suffering from overkill by other candidates." Since I did not have the money to enter even one primary, it was unthinkable to enter two at once; I decided to concentrate what resources I could on Florida. A good showing there— which to me meant 5 or 6 percent—would establish me as a serious candidate, and perhaps a little money would start coming in.

Everybody was eying Florida in the same frame of mind. Lindsay hoped it would be his springboard into serious contention. Senator Edmund S. Muskie hoped it would demonstrate that he was so far in front that he could not be denied. Senator Hubert H. Humphrey hoped he would show he was still the vote-getter of yore. Senator George S. McGovern wanted to snag a few delegates to show that he was not poison in the South. Senator Henry M. Jackson was out to show the country that the other candidates were all too far left for the voters and that somebody like Jackson was what they really wanted. Finally, there was Governor George C. Wallace of Alabama, who was resolutely refusing to run again as a third-party candidate. He was sure, with good reason, that Florida would be the first of a string of victories that would make him a man to be reckoned with at the Democratic convention in July.

By any normal, reasonable standards my decision to enter such a crowded field of candidates was not sensible. Florida seemed to be predominantly Wallace country in 1972: what liberal votes there were in Miami, Jacksonville and other cities would be split among the field of contenders, and the most I could expect would be one of the smaller splinters. But if I had been reasonable about such things, I would not have run anywhere; in every state there was some reason not to enter. California and Massachusetts were both winner-take-all states. Other states were like Florida, Wisconsin and New Jersey, where the winner in each Congressional District picked up all the votes for the district; it would be possible for me to get 6, 10, even 20 percent statewide and not have a single delegate to show for it. But all of that seemed to me only another facet of the system I was out to shake up, and we weren't going to shake it up unless we got out and ran. The strategy was to plunge in and see what happened. Either the support came together or it didn't; either the money to make the effort meaningful came in or it didn't; but nothing would happen unless we made a try.

There were a lot of people in Florida who wanted me to come in, and that was the reason I had to go. One of the first was Gwen Cherry of Miami, the lawyer already mentioned, whom I had met while we were both active in organizing the National Women's Political Caucus early in 1971. She telephoned me in Washington and said she was talking with other black leaders and with women in the women's movement, and that Chisholm for President organizations were ready to swing into action in several parts of the state if I would say the word. Gwen Cherry said she would do everything she could to help me. "I think," she told a newspaper reporter, "she will do particularly well here, better than in other areas, because of the fact we have a larger percentage of women voters. I think they will support the gesture, whether they support the candidate or not." Gwen admitted to an Orlando *Star* writer that I couldn't win, but she said, "I think she's very, very generous to put herself forward as a candidate, because she's going to make some of the other candidates address themselves to the human priorities of life."

Except for Gwen Cherry, black elected officials in Florida did not show any enthusiasm for the idea of my running. One would-be officeholder, Alcee Hastings, a Fort Lauderdale lawyer who ran for the State Senate in 1970 and entertained hopes of trying for some higher office, launched a sharp and entirely gratuitous attack on me. The only explanation for it I have ever found is that he might have been hoping to be Florida's black favorite-son candidate, à la Julian Bond; back in October he had declared that black political caucuses were being planned in Pensacola, Jacksonville, Daytona, Tampa and Miami to consider naming favorite-son candidates, and it was "a distinct possibility" he would be the choice. My entry might thwart his plan, he may have felt. At any rate, he started predicting that Florida blacks would not support Mrs. Chisholm, and "she would get the heck beaten out of her in this state." Worse than that, he said, "She will embarrass a lot of her own people who have already made commitments to other candidates. She hasn't done her homework, and she is simply not known in Florida," he concluded.

The attack did not unsettle me, coming as it did from a

man I did not know and, indeed, had never heard of. My first reaction was that, like other blacks in politics, Mr. Hastings had hidden motives for attacking me, one of them being my sex, and that he did not understand the basic fact that my candidacy was not based on blackness. He, like many others, was "hung up" on blackness and could not grasp that I was not in the field as the black candidate, or as the woman candidate, but that I saw myself as the candidate of all Americans.

Remus Allen, a dedicated young Tallahassee lawyer, was one of my first recruits. He saw the implications for the political future of blacks in Florida if they were able to show their strength by uniting around my candidacy. His help in handling details of filing slates and his inspired detail work in canvassing voters in northern Florida turned out to be invaluable; in fact, his were some of the most professional and effective efforts in the whole campaign. In northern Florida's major city, Jacksonville, a young anti-poverty worker named Isaiah Williams took the lead and, working closely with Remus Allen, made north Florida an unexpectedly bright spot in the campaign. Originally, it had seemed probable that my strength, if any, would be concentrated in Tampa and Miami. But both cities turned out to be disappointments, largely because of a problem that was to plague me from start to finish: supporters from various groups, blacks, white students, white women and so on, all individually eager, competed jealously for leading roles and proved unable to work effectively together. I went into Florida with what I thought was the nucleus of a campaign organization; by the time the primary was over it had crumbled to pieces. A major reason was a lack of experienced, competent professionals in the national campaign office; eager but inexperienced volunteers were trying to do the work but could not possibly handle it all; there was no money to hire anybody else, and inevitably the campaign was to limp from crisis to crisis in state after state.

Going into Florida I had a national campaign manager, Gerald Robinson, who was hired out to me from a political public relations firm. After a month, he resigned in disillusionment over the problem of trying to put together a state campaign organization out of the confused mess of squabbling groups he had to work with, combined with the frustrations of having nobody in Washington to back him up with clear decisions on what to do, and staff work to follow through on doing it. Gerry wrote me a letter pointing out the problems we were having because I was trying to function as a campaign manager as well as being the candidate, while at the same time trying to hold up my end as a member of Congress. The result, he said, was "the appearance of a shoddy and poorly organized campaign structure which turns people off, and loss of support from people who would have otherwise supported the campaign."

The problems were with basic things like answering letters in Washington, getting brochures and bumper stickers and buttons into the hands of the workers in Florida, and arranging schedules without conflicts, so they could be adhered to. Gerry and two outstanding young white men who, working completely without pay, formed the total of my state-wide campaign staff in Florida, found it a hopeless task. Worse yet, they had to take all the flak for the trouble, very little of which was their fault.

The two young men were Robert Gottleib, a brilliant twenty-one-year-old Cornell senior, and Roger Barr, a Floridian who was not much older. Roger, I learned later, is an expert tennis player; he taught tennis at a Tampa area club for ten days to raise $300 and planned to live on that until the campaign was over. Roger detested shoes and usually wore only a pair of shorts and an old shirt; but he was the most committed and hard-working young man I have ever seen. He stayed with me clear through the New York primary on June 20. Some middle-class people, black and white, tried to tell me that "that raga-muffin white boy" was hurting the campaign with his appearance. Roger was aware of this and stayed in the background in some situations, but dressing the way he wanted to dress was a point of honor with him, and I understood and accepted that. If I could have had twenty volunteers like him, it would have made an incalculable difference. Bob Gottleib, who had never seen Florida before, was trying to make up with intelligence and energy what he lacked in age and experience; he zipped around the state trying to get feuding groups together, delivering materials and making plans for my pre-primary state campaign tour.

My Florida campaign consisted of two tours, one of five

days early in January—before I had formally announced but after I had finally resolved to run—and one of six days the week before the primary. Miami was the first stop on the first tour; I spent January 4 there, a day of interviews with TV and newspaper reporters, punctuated at noon with a luncheon speech at the Tiger Bay Club, a men's luncheon club that had never—or so I was told—had a woman speaker, and had had quite a discussion about it before I was invited. They had a 100 percent turnout of their members, a rare thing, they said. The audience was all white, businessmen, presumably conservative. I had just finished the first of several position papers that would come out during the campaign. It was on foreign policy, and I made it the basis of my talk. When I stressed that the plight of the Palestinian refugees is the primary concern we should have in the Middle East, some of the audience decided I was pro-Arab. During the question period they pressed me on the point and would not be convinced that I was neither pro-Arab nor pro-Israeli; in their minds, I had to be one or the other. They would not see that what I was saying was that the trouble in the situation results in large part from the cruel way these refugees have been ignored by everyone involved—Arab, Israeli, American and Russian—for more than twenty years, and that U.S. foreign policy should avoid taking sides, focus on the true human tragedy, and try to deal with that.

In the evening the Miami Chisholm organization held a fund-raising chicken box supper in the Bay Front Auditorium, and the next day I flew to Tampa, with a stopover to speak at West Palm Beach. At Tampa the day's main event was a speech at a Democratic Women's Club meeting in a large church; the Tampa woman who made the arrangements put her whole family on the dais, to the visible irritation of others in the campaign organization there. It was the first of a string of similar incidents that would nearly paralyze the Tampa campaign with interpersonal friction. On to Tallahassee. Remus Allen met me at the airport, and it was straight to Florida State University for the first big Southern student audience of the campaign. I expected the white students to be cool, even hostile; instead I was surprised by their warm response, and by the turnout—there must have been two thousand there.

When I talked to the students, I got another shock. My expectation was that John Lindsay would be extremely popular among college-age people, and that he and I would be—as Lindsay feared—in direct competition for the black and youth votes. But the students had nothing good to say about Lindsay. "He's a handsome phony," one said. "I've seen him on the Dick Cavett show," said another, "and you can tell he's shallow." It was McGovern, Wallace and Chisholm that the students went for, and in straw polls at several campuses, I was usually number two, whichever of the male candidates was first.

Remus took me to the State Capitol for a press conference, where I answered the same questions I had in Miami and Tampa. "Are you a serious candidate?" "If you know you can't win, why are you running?" "Which of the major candidates do you favor?" In my own ears, I sounded like a broken record. They introduced me to the Florida Secretary of State, who told me in detail the legal requirements of the primary, and said he was very glad I was running. I was introduced to Reubin Askew, the most gracious governor I met in the South; there was a banquet, then the next morning a press breakfast and another campus speech, at Florida A & M. Like most poor candidates, I did a lot of speaking at colleges; the halls are free and the audiences responsive. If you don't have money to hire an auditorium and turn out a crowd to fill it, a college is the answer.

Over to Pensacola for a speech Remus had arranged, then across the state to Jacksonville. I felt like a real candidate; he had set up dates, arranged transportation, taken care of advance work like a professional. In Jacksonville, Ike Williams had outdone himself; a ninety-car motorcade was blocking the airport roads. There were more whites than blacks. I went over to talk to a white man who was wearing a straw hat emblazoned "Chizm for President." "You spelled my name wrong," I chided him. "That doesn't matter!" he said. "I want you for President!" The motorcade delivered us at Edward Waters College for a city-wide youth rally, with another crowd of two thousand or more. A reception, a TV interview, a banquet, breakfast with the League of Women Voters and the National Organization for Women and, last, a fund-raising rally at a Methodist church. I came back to Washington on January 9 elated. Perhaps I had no money for transportation, television and staff, but it seemed that I had things money couldn't buy—hard-working volunteers and an enthusiastic reception almost everywhere I went.

As my campaign schedule fell together (to say that it was planned would be laughable) there was to be only one more trip to Florida, although I did make a flying trip back at the insistence of the Tampa group to appear at the Florida State Fair early in February. All I did there was walk around and introduce myself. Some of the eight hundred or more people whose hands I shook congratulated me, others laughed. One old white man, to whom I said, "Hello, I'm Shirley Chisholm and I'm running for President," drew back and looked at me suspiciously. "You're *what?*" he asked.

Before the second campaign tour in Florida, which was the week before the March 14 primary, the simmering busing issue had been brought to a boil in the state. It was done, I am convinced, by Wallace supporters, who seized on a court decision involving the Richmond, Virginia, area to fan the flames of racial fear and stampede white Florida voters to their candidate. If it was a Wallace strategy, it worked extremely well. The Alabama governor had been the favorite in Florida from the start, but during February it grew clear that he would be not just a winner, but a big winner. Over Governor Askew's objections, the state legislature had put a referendum question dealing with school busing for desegregation on the primary ballot, and excitement over this ran high in the weeks just before the primary. Eventually, Askew went on television with a soberly eloquent plea to his people not to turn the clock back and undo all the progress the South had made toward racial equality. The appearance increased national awareness of Askew as one of the South's progressive new leaders, but failed to sway the voters. The whole affair probably had little effect on my showing in the final vote, unless it may have driven a few black voters here and there to support me, as they witnessed the white candidates making double-talk on the issues, not excluding Hubert Humphrey.

On both my Florida tours, someone in nearly every crowd asked me what I thought about busing. The truth is I have never been a strong advocate of busing, as the bureaucrats put it, "to correct racial imbalance." The root cause of segregated schools is racism—economic and social discrimination against dark-skinned citizens. One school is crowded with black children because their parents have been herded into that neighborhood by the bigoted white majority; busing some of the blacks to a white school is not doing anything to erase the real problem. The only good I could ever see in it was the chance that, when white children in turn are bused into formerly black schools, the school board would suddenly see the wisdom of improving those schools and giving them a fair share of the annual budget. But in the atmosphere that pervaded Florida during the primary, there was no way I could give comfort to the racists by appearing to agree with them.

"Busing," I told audience after audience, "is an artificial way of solving the segregation problem." Open housing is the real answer, I said. But as long as the problem exists, an artificial solution is better than none. Then I would let them have it. "Where were you," I asked the whites, "when for years black children were being bused out of their neighborhoods and carried miles on old rattletrap buses to go down back roads to a dirty school with a tarpaper roof and no toilets? If you believed in neighborhood schools, where were you then? I'm not going to shed any crocodile tears for you now that you've discovered the busing problem." If there was any other candidate in the Florida primary who was taking a similarly strong stand in the face of the public agitation over the phony busing issue, I have yet to read about it. Jackson lined up with Wallace; Humphrey took so many stands that no one could pin him down, but the impression he left was that he was against busing; McGovern, Lindsay and Muskie equivocated. It was a sorry performance, and one that George Wallace did not fail to seize on—all the Northern liberals suddenly talking out of both sides of their mouths when they came down South looking for votes. Shirley Chisholm, he was to say repeatedly, was the only other candidate who said the same things in the South that she said in the North.

Between the two Florida swings, my campaign organization in Florida all but fell apart. Without any money from me, and lacking an experienced director after Gerry Robinson left, local volunteers out of sheer enthusiasm tried to get something together. Conflicts between factions nearly halted the Tampa and Miami efforts; blacks versus whites, men versus women. Muskie, Lindsay, Humphrey and

Jackson were pouring about half a million dollars each into the campaign. In the end, I would spend less than $10,000. It was all I had; there was no alternative to depending on volunteers. Besides, I kept hoping that somehow all the disorganized, disregarded elements in the electorate would come together; how, I didn't know, but it seemed to me that my candidacy was the only way they had to express their frustration. "Her primary campaign," the Daytona Beach *News-Journal* observed, "really consists of nothing but a belief in the people and just plain faith." We never did lack for eager volunteers, but there was no one who could give them clear-cut directions. Some work was duplicated while other chores were left undone. The national office in Washington was in the same plight. In the confusion, local jealousies and rivalries thrived. Compared with the professional and well-financed campaigns of the other candidates, mine did not inspire confidence. There were countless damaging results; a trip to St. Petersburg was rescheduled five times and finally canceled four days before the last date agreed on, but no one in Tampa thought to tell the St. Petersburg *Times,* and its reporter went out and waited for me to arrive. It was not a good way to treat one of the state's leading newspapers. In Miami there were similar disasters. We learned later that some high school history teachers had sent students out to canvass for me, but the office there knew nothing about it. On one Miami stop there was a press conference at the Vizcaya Restaurant, but someone called the radio stations and said it was the Vizcaya Gardens, with the result that no one came to the press conference. Muskie was whistle-stopping through the state in a six-car train, Lindsay was traveling in a cavalcade of buses, and Humphrey was using a chartered airplane, while I went from place to place in commercial airliners and volunteers' automobiles. While their appearances were advanced by experts, mine were publicized by notices on church bulletin boards and phone calls to newspapers and broadcasting stations.

Thanks to Spanish classes in college and years of contact with Spanish-speaking neighbors in Brooklyn, I speak that language fairly fluently, and this, I thought, might win me support with the Miami area community of Cuban refugees. What I did not know was that many of the ex-Cubans are members of the pre-revolutionary middle and upper classes and are staunch conservatives who, if they did risk involvement in American politics, would normally align themselves with the Republican right wing. I went to Ybor City, where a number of ex-Cubans live; through another of those maddening slip-ups by my volunteers no one had been told I was coming. In Miami, I joined sugar-cane workers on a picket line and addressed them in Spanish: "None of the other candidates who come here are from you. I am from you, I am of you, I understand." The response was not what I had hoped.

The Miami scene in my campaign was dominated by white women activists, who were frequently at odds with workers from the black community, a problem that would dog me in California and wherever the women's movement was strong. The women were hard, tireless workers, good at arranging television and newspaper publicity, and very committed—but primarily to the feminist issues of the campaign. They wanted to talk of little but abortion, day care, equal rights and other women's issues. Disgruntled blacks complained to me that they could not relate to the campaign coordinators. They insisted on dealing with me directly. "You're the candidate," they said. "You're supposed to be the candidate of the people. Why can't we get to you?" I had to spend time with them, trying to smooth things out, and with the feminists, trying to convince them that there was more to the campaign than their concerns. But feminist advocacy turned out to be a very hard element to combine with coalition politics. The women were politically naïve; they were enthusiastic, but they did not understand the first thing about politics. Even more than blacks, I think, they showed the effects of their past exclusion from the political process, and unlike blacks, they find it hard to believe that they have a great deal to learn.

Still I felt confident that I would surprise everyone; it was not the first time I had been counted out in advance, only to win. My first campaign for the New York Assembly, and my first Congressional campaign against James Farmer, former national director of the Congress of Racial Equality, had both been carried on against what the experts thought insurmountable odds, and each time, on Election Day, it turned out that I had been the strongest candidate all along. The large, enthusiastic crowds that I drew made me keep up my hope. If I finished fourth or fifth, or even sixth, I felt I would have shown once again that the experts don't know everything about what the people really think and what they want.

Late in the evening of March 8, six days before the primary, I flew to Jacksonville. Once more Ike Williams and Remus Allen had done a near-professional job of planning and advancing a campaign tour in northern Florida. There was a crowded two-day round of appearances in and around Jacksonville—visits to black-run businesses, speeches at colleges and public rallies, interviews with newspaper and television reporters. On the Saturday before the primary Remus had laid out a trip that some of my closest associates back home were concerned about—through the Florida Panhandle, known to some people as "South Georgia," the real Wallace country. Remus was convinced that the black vote there—a majority in some spots and a large minority in others—could be mine if I went there and showed that I was really running to win. I felt that, whether this was true or not, it would be a worthwhile move if it could increase the dialogue between blacks and whites, minimize the growing polarization between the races, and open up their attitudes. About fifty people from back home, Bedford-Stuyvesant in Brooklyn, came down to join us, led by City Councilman William Thompson. We chartered a bus in Tallahassee and christened it the Chisholm Express. With packed lunches and stacks of campaign literature, buttons and bumper stickers, we set out in mid-morning for Quincy, where I was to speak on the courthouse square.

The sun was hot and we drove over miles of dusty country roads, through small towns that were just clusters of gas stations, stores and bungalows, past little farms. Quincy is a city of about 40,000 and is 60 percent black. The Reverend Ralph Abernathy met us there. "A few years ago," he told the crowd of about a thousand blacks, leavened by a few whites, "we could not have stood here on the steps of this courthouse and had this kind of a rally." He said McGovern and Lindsay were good men, and he would give them grades of B, but Mrs. Chisholm was the only candidate in Tuesday's primary who deserved an A, "for Able." There were loud cheers, and I was surprised to see even some of the older blacks in the crowd raise their fists in a black power salute. I had never seen so many old black people in one of my audiences. Many were seventy-five and eighty years old, and they had apparently come for miles to the rally. They could not have had much notice. We did not advance our Panhandle trip too much because of fear of arousing counter-demonstrations. Quincy and Marianna had both been the scenes of protest marches not long ago, and we did not want to touch off new disturbances. There were none, in any case; the only incident I heard of was innocent. A few black boys went around town ripping Wallace stickers off car bumpers and replacing them with Chisholm ones.

Dr. Abernathy's statement of support was not made on behalf of the Southern Christian Leadership Conference, which never endorsed me or anyone else. As a matter of fact, it was not an endorsement from him either, merely an expression of solidarity and goodwill.

We went on to Marianna, and as we rode I could not help seeing how poor the country was. I knew the figures: the population had shrunk by 5 percent in the last twenty years; agriculture was eroding away and was not being replaced by industry; the brunt of its effects fell on the poor black population, although many whites were little better off. But seeing the poverty of rural black Southerners close up made the statistics seem understated.

Marianna had not seen a Presidential candidate since 1951, but on that day it saw two. George Wallace was scheduled to appear the same night. Our bus went to the courthouse square again, and burly, polite sheriff's deputies escorted me to the steps. The crowd was perhaps about three hundred, nearly all black; a few whites stood out on the fringes of the audience. Later in the day, Wallace, whose tour was being heavily covered by national reporters and TV crews, drew about five hundred white voters to the same spot.

As I stood on the steps and started to speak, I thought about the Civil War. Nearby, as everywhere in the South, there was a statue of a Confederate soldier. Moss hung from the branches. The day was hot. The rifle the statue was holding seemed almost to be pointing at me. A feeling came over me about the courthouse, a place of fear for blacks for a hundred years, where white justice had been dealt out to them. "I never thought I'd live to see a black person speaking from the courthouse steps," one old black man told me later. When I talked about the need for coming together, the crowd responded with mixed emotions, some with laughter and some with tears.

Panama City, Pensacola, up for a church women's breakfast in Thomasville, Georgia, then back to Tallahassee. There were speeches at Florida A & M and Florida State University that Sunday, and the students asked me what I planned to do about protecting the environment. To them, "ecology" was almost the shibboleth that busing was to their elders. I let them have it straight, too. "How can I be worried about the threat to the mammals in the remote oceans?" I asked. "The real environmental problem is in the slums where people live surrounded by garbage and their children eat the peeling chips of lead paint and are bitten by rats. There is your environmental problem. Let's do something about the children first, and then worry about the whales."

At the motel in Jacksonville where our party stayed was a group of Lindsay workers. Perhaps it would be better to call them Lindsay employees. My people said they saw them in the bar all day long and heard they were running up tremendous tabs and room-service bills. If that was the story everywhere, no wonder Lindsay was showing so little results from his half-million-dollar outlay, I thought. It was awful what they did to him. Back in New York I had kept hearing, "You can't find anyone at City Hall. Lindsay has them all in Florida." Then in Florida, we saw them living it up. They had no commitment to their candidate. The people involved were not Lindsay's top staff, who were dedicated to him and worked hard; the culprits were second- and third-level city employees who seemed to be just out for a good time.

Perhaps they had started out working hard and given up. Everywhere in Florida Lindsay met tremendous opposition and personal attacks of a viciousness that no one else felt. Citizens of New York City went south to work against him, concentrating on ex-city residents, many of them Jewish. They used posters, banners, buttons, even sky-writing. The theme was "He can't run New York—how could he run the country?" When I became aware that some of my people were joining in and heckling Lindsay rallies, I told them to stop it. We were opponents, but we were not enemies. I wanted no part of those tactics.

Some of Lindsay's closest associates feel that if I had not run, he would have drawn the 4 percent of the vote that I wound up with, giving him more than 10 percent and keeping his candidacy alive. It is a baseless theory. What beat Lindsay in Florida was the voters' perception that he was trying to use the state to save his political life. The opposition of his enemies from New York City and the betrayal of some of his campaign staff did not help, but basically Lindsay was never in it; he had no chance from the start. It was not the place, and it was not the year, for a handsome liberal to wage a slick media campaign.

VII

She's Just a Stalking-Horse

AFTER THE FIRST Florida campaign trip, it was time for me to make an honest woman of myself. I called a press conference for January 25, 1972, to make my formal announcement, in Brooklyn's biggest Baptist church. Conrad was there, Mac Holder, my chief political strategist, and my whole Brooklyn office staff, representatives of community organizations, and even a dozen or fifteen people from Maine who had come down to try to interest me in entering the Maine primary. (I resisted their pleas successfully for once.) The church was packed with television cameras and lights, reporters and well-wishers.

"I stand before you today as a candidate for the Democratic nomination for the Presidency of the United States," I said. "I am not the candidate of black America, although I am black and proud. I am not the candidate of the women's movement of this country, although I am a woman, and I am equally proud of that. I am not the candidate of any political bosses or special interests. . . . I am the candidate of the people.

"We Americans," I said, "are a dynamic people because of our rugged individuality and our cherished diversity, because of our belief in human dignity, because of our generosity and goodwill to our fellow men, and most importantly, because of our tradition of moving forward to actively confront those problems which plague us in a world growing more complex each year.

"Like all human beings, we have made mistakes. Our involvement in Vietnam was, and remains at this very moment, a terrible tragedy. To have intervened in the civil war in that country, and to have intervened in still two more countries, Laos and Cambodia, was an ill-conceived blunder whose consequences all of us have had to suffer. To leave our men there, or to increase massive bombing in the process of withdrawing them, is to compound the havoc and misery which we are inflicting on the people of Indochina, our young men who have been killed and mutilated and rendered drug addicts, and ourselves, whose hard-earned money has, during a serious economic recession, made up the billions of dollars spent in Vietnam when we so urgently need these resources at home. . . .

"Beyond Vietnam and its horrors, which have dominated our newspapers and television for eight long years, and beyond the economic recession, which has caused severe hardship to so many Americans, is the visible, ongoing destruction of our natural environment and our loss of a sense of personal security in our daily lives. Perhaps even more fundamental is our loss of the feeling of community, shock at the continuing injustices and inequities in the land we love, our suspicions of pervasive incompetence and corruption, our feeling that there is an absence of respectable authority in the nation, and our loss of confidence in ourselves, with apathy or despair arising from the conviction that we are powerless to make ourselves heard or felt in remedying our ills.

"We have looked in vain to the Nixon administration for the courage, the spirit, the character and the words to lift us, to bring out the best in us, to rekindle in each of us our faith in the American dream. All that we have received in return is just another smooth exercise in political manipulation, deceit and deception, callousness and indifference to our individual problems, and the disgusting playing of divisive politics, pitting young against old, labor against management, North against South, and black against white. The abiding concern of this administration has been one of political expediency rather than the needs of man's nature."

But, I said, I had not lost faith in the American people. "I believe that we are smart enough to correct our mistakes. I believe we are intelligent enough to recognize the talent, energy and dedication which all Americans, including women and minorities, have to offer. I know, from my travels to the cities and small towns of America, that we have a vast potential, hitherto neglected, which can and must be put to constructive use in getting our great nation together. I know that millions of Americans from all walks of life agree with me that leadership does not mean putting the ear to the ground, to follow public opinion, but to have the vision of what is necessary and the courage to make it possible—not by force, violence or intimidation, but by persuasion, example and law. We must turn away from the control of the prosaic, the privileged, and the old-line, tired politicians to open our society to the energies and abilities of countless new groups of Americans—women, blacks, browns, Indians, Orientals and youth—so that they can develop their own full potential, and thereby participate equally and enthusiastically in building a strong and just society, rich in its diversity and noble in its quality of life."

There was one crashing understatement in my announcement speech, when I said, "I stand here without the endorsements of any big-name politicians or celebrities." I could almost have said that the political powers were all arrayed against me. Manhattan Borough President Percy Sutton was an exception; he endorsed me early in the campaign and eventually made my nominating speech in Miami. Representatives Ron Dellums of California and Parren Mitchell of Maryland appeared with me at a Washington press conference at which I repeated my announcement that I was officially in the race. Both Dellums and Mitchell backed me strongly from the beginning. Representative Charles Rangel of Harlem gave me his best wishes but was not in a position to make it an open endorsement; he was in a tough reelection campaign, and to endorse me would have been to risk alienating the support he needed from people who were endorsing other candidates.

One surprise came from my sister Congresswoman from New York, Bella Abzug. By mistake, she had not been sent an invitation either to the Brooklyn or to the Washington press conference, and my office began to get calls the day before the announcement from Bella's office and from the National Women's Political Caucus office, frantically urging me to invite her, and saying that she was deeply offended at having been left out. We sent telegrams of invitation to her offices in New York and Washington. She did not appear in Brooklyn, but about five minutes before the Washington press conference started I had a call from an Abzug aide asking whether Bella could appear with me and my supporters at the event. I could not discover whether she intended to endorse me, or what she had in mind, but I said yes because I could see no reason to say no. After my statement, Mitchell and Dellums spoke; they gave me strong and moving endorsements. Then Bella made a strange statement, largely about movements and the underprivileged in politics. She said little about my candidacy, except that it was "an idea whose time has come," if I remember correctly.

Later a reporter asked her whether she had endorsed me or not. Bella hedged. She said she supported "the idea" of my candidacy and would support me in those states where I was running (at the time she appeared to think I was going into only three or four primaries). Bella never offered to campaign for me in Florida, North Carolina or even New

York, for that matter. It was a letdown, and also bewildering: if she intended to sit on the fence, why did she ask to appear with me when I made my announcement for the Presidency?

There were other leaders of the National Women's Political Caucus who were not so equivocal. I had no thought of asking the NWPC for its support as an organization, for several reasons, although I was urged repeatedly to go to a caucus board meeting and make my case. But I did not want to embarrass any of the other board members; some of them were Republicans who, although deeply concerned with women's issues, were going to support Richard Nixon. One, LaDonna Harris, was the wife of another candidate, Senator Fred Harris of Oklahoma, although he dropped out early. Another, Liz Carpenter, former press secretary to Lady Bird Johnson, told me that because of past loyalties she was supporting Hubert Humphrey. But Liz, a tireless worker for the NWPC and the women's movement, helped me throughout the campaign in other ways. She encouraged reporters, with whom she has extensive contacts, to cover my campaign and listen to what I had to say on the issues. She called Ben Bradlee, managing editor of the Washington *Post*, and suggested that *Post* editors hold a background session with me as they had with Muskie, Humphrey and other candidates. And she let me use her name in several Washington-area fund-raising efforts, and came to some of the events herself.

The National Organization for Women (NOW) could

not endorse any political candidate, because it would lose its tax-exempt status if it did. However, Wilma Scott Heide, NOW's national president, did endorse me personally. She worked long and hard for me, speaking and helping to set up speaking appearances for me, and wore at least fifteen Chisholm buttons wherever she went.

Jo-Ann Evans Gardner, a Pittsburgh psychologist who is a member of the NWPC board, a long-time activist in the women's movement, although enrolled as a Republican, threw herself into my campaign. Joining with Alma Fox, a black woman active in Democratic politics, the NAACP and other civil rights groups, she organized a Chisholm for President chapter in Pittsburgh, held fund-raisers and helped line up delegate candidates in Pennsylvania.

Two of the most prominent members of the women's movement and the NWPC, Betty Friedan and Gloria Steinem, wound up supporting me and running (unsuccessfully) as Chisholm delegates in Manhattan. But before they settled down in my corner, they went through some maneuvers that baffled me. Betty was an enthusiast for my candidacy from the start—even before the start. In mid-1971, she urged me to make my announcement on August 26, Women's Day. But Betty had been a McCarthy supporter in 1968, and later on, when McCarthy was somewhat tentatively running again, she told me that although she fully supported me and would campaign for me, she wanted to campaign for Gene in primaries where he was running and I was not. I explained that such a double endorsement would only enhance the problems I was having in being taken seriously as a candidate, and urged her to support either me or McCarthy.

Something of the same indecision seemed to afflict Gloria. The charming, dynamic editor of *Ms.* magazine is often on television talk shows as a spokeswoman for the women's movement, and naturally she began to be asked whom she supported for President. She would say, "I'm for Shirley Chisholm—but I think that George McGovern is the best of the *male* candidates." This hybrid endorsement began to exasperate me, and finally, after she had done it again on a television program in Chicago on which we both appeared, I told her, "Gloria, you're supporting either George McGovern or Shirley Chisholm. I don't mind if you are supporting George. If he is your candidate, so be it, but don't do me any favors by giving me this semi-endorsement. I don't need that kind of help."

Some of the black and brown women on the NWPC Policy Council became the strongest and most valuable supporters I had—Fannie Lou Hamer, Lupe Anguiano, Gwen Cherry and Carol Taylor, among others. They did not have the one problem with my candidacy that many white women did: the whites knew I couldn't be elected, and so their support, even when it was given, seemed a little tentative, because they felt they were fighting for a lost cause. But women like Fannie Lou, Lupe and the rest, having been long active in the civil rights movement and other minority causes, were used to taking up seemingly impossible challenges. Their whole experience had taught them that they might not win the ultimate objective, but they would make some gains and in the process increase the chance that success would come, someday.

Apart from the women's movement, much of which surprised me with its coolness to my candidacy, I began to encounter outright hostility from some state and local party officials and local black leaders. In Tallahassee, on my second trip to Florida, I was to encounter a black pastor who refused to let me speak at his church. "We've got Hubert Humphrey," he said. "We don't need you." In North Carolina, the opposition came from blacks committed to Terry Sanford; in other states it was to be from McGovern supporters, reaching a peak of acrimony during the California primary and again during the convention.

Former Governor Terry Sanford of North Carolina, the president of Duke University, was out to keep his state from going for George C. Wallace. There were people in the state who wanted me to run; I said I would, but they would have to provide the money and organization. Even more than in Florida, it developed into a chaos of misunderstanding, cross-purposes and hurt feelings. Sanford, a liberal who had done great things for his state's educational system and started programs to attack poverty before the federal government did, did not want to see his state's votes go to Wallace. He arranged to be "drafted" as a favorite son, hoping to hold North Carolina for Humphrey, Muskie or some other moderate candidate. Humphrey, Muskie and the rest decided to stay out; their entry would probably have split the non-Wallace vote and handed the state to Wallace. At first, Sanford and his backers did not seem very worried about me. They could see that my organization was loose, amateurish and impoverished; they paid no attention to me until late in April, about three weeks before the May 6 primary, when it began to appear that even though I had made very little personal effort in the state, I was going to get a significant slice of the vote.

In March, April and May I was campaigning in New Jersey, Massachusetts, Minnesota, California, Michigan and North Carolina. But my campaign trips were mostly in the form of a day here and a day there, a weekend in this state, and one in that one. For most of the primary months, I tried to campaign without cutting seriously into the time I spent in Washington taking care of Congressional business. I flew back and forth across the country, trying to be a candidate and a Congresswoman simultaneously; it was a frustrating and ultimately impossible thing to attempt. When I had to cancel speeches and appearances at fund-raisers and rallies, the local campaign workers who had put their time and money into arranging the events were naturally upset. Several times an event would be canceled, rescheduled, canceled and rescheduled again. After a while no adequate excuse could be offered, and more than one eager supporter became alienated. In Wisconsin, for instance, my state coordinator, the Reverend Gene Boutlier, became so frustrated at this kind of occurrence that he resigned shortly before the election and joined the McGovern campaign. He had been afraid of the showing that Wallace would make in Wisconsin and felt that since I was not available to campaign personally—as it worked out, I never set foot in Wisconsin although I was on the ballot there—he might better devote his efforts to bolstering McGovern's campaign. To some of my rank-and-file supporters, it may have seemed that I was closing up shop and endorsing McGovern.

The trouble was that I felt my first responsibility was to be on the floor of the House, or in the Education and Labor Committee, when important votes were taken, and legislative business kept coming up, unpredictably, and conflicting with campaign dates set long in advance. As it was, the number of votes I missed to campaign was worrying me, although I believe I never missed one in which my vote or presence would have been crucial.

In New Jersey, I campaigned in nearly every county of the thirteen in which I was entered, without winning a delegate. But some of the slates entered for me did make respectable showings, and it is curious that, in a preference poll on the New Jersey ballot, a nonbinding "beauty contest" in which only Terry Sanford and I were entered, a total of 51,344 persons picked me as their choice for President. Sanford got 25,401 votes. This was out of close to half a million voting; most people apparently did not pay any attention to the Presidential choice line. The delegates elected were nearly all for McGovern, with a sprinkling of uncommitted regular Democrats. My campaign in New Jersey was coordinated by a brilliant young Princeton student from Arkansas, Marion Humphreys, who had worked as an intern in my Washington office and volunteered—in the midst of finishing school—to help try to get Chisholm organizations set up in as many New Jersey counties as possible.

An important legal precedent was set during my campaign, through the work of a young public service lawyer, Tom Asher of the Media Service Project in Washington, D.C. During the weeks just before the California primary, Hubert H. Humphrey had challenged George McGovern to a series of television debates. Somehow (and I am not sure the full story of how it happened ever became public) the three networks—CBS, ABC and NBC—wound up donating their weekly half-hour public affairs interview programs to the two candidates. "Meet the Press," "Face the Nation" and "Issues and Answers" were all stretched to an hour and rescheduled to provide, in effect, three one-hour debates between Humphrey and McGovern during the last full week before the California primary. Tom Asher filed a protest on my behalf with the Federal Communications Commission, citing section 315 of the Federal Communications Act, which says that if any broadcasting station permits itself to be used by any legally qualified candidate for an office, it must permit equal opportunities to all other candidates. The networks claimed that the three programs were regular interview shows, and exempt from the rule. The Federal Communications Commission upheld the networks, and Asher went to the U.S. Court of Appeals.

Within hours after the FCC ruling, the court issued an order reversing the commission and ordering ABC and CBS each to provide me with one half-hour of prime air time. NBC had conceded earlier and scheduled me on one half-hour of its morning program, "Today."

In the Wisconsin primary, early in April, in spite of my absence from the state campaign, I drew more than 9,100 votes, the bulk from Milwaukee and Dane County. That was less than 1 percent, but it was more than the voters gave Representative Wilbur D. Mills, Representative Patsy T. Mink of Hawaii, Los Angeles Mayor Samuel Yorty, or Indiana Senator Vance Hartke. McGovern won it, but Wallace was a strong second, ahead of Humphrey.

Entering the Massachusetts primary was a spur-of-the-moment decision. While I was making my first California tour I got an excited phone call from two would-be supporters, James Pitts and Saundra Graham, a Cambridge council-woman. They said they were sure that if I spent some time in the Boston area there was an excellent opportunity for me to pick up some delegates. They urged me to fly east for a caucus to be held the next day, a Saturday. It was impossible for me to attend the meeting, a New Democratic Coalition convention in Worcester, but in spite of that I got 23 percent of the vote, a surprise even to my backers. McGovern, who got 62 percent, had a strong, hard-working organization which had been in existence for some time, and Senator Eugene McCarthy, who also had organized support, drew only 13 percent. My support had apparently sprung up suddenly during the week before the liberal Democrats' meeting. Jim and Saundra, excited about the results, came to see me in Brooklyn, with charts and figures to show where the potential Chisholm strength was in Massachusetts. We decided to concentrate on the districts where I had a chance and not worry about the rest of the state. Jim Pitts plunged into the campaign with a verve and dedication that astonished me; it was support like that I got, all unsought, from him and Saundra that made me feel it was perhaps going to be worthwhile to press on with the campaign. They set up an itinerary and, just before the April 25 primary, I spent three days there.

One of the first speeches was to a Spanish-speaking group at Cardinal Cushing High School in Boston. I gave it in Spanish and strolled afterward through a bazaar that was being held. The response was enthusiastic; none of the "major" candidates was able to communicate with these voters in their own language and make them feel understood in return. We went to a big shopping center in Roxbury for a hand-shaking tour, then to the Charles Street A.M.E. Church for a rally. It was Sunday afternoon. Just as the rally was about to begin, there was a stir of excitement at the back of the church. Several young men dressed in women's clothing were making a grand but noisy entrance. They were members of the Gay Liberation movement, come in drag to support me. One wore a beautiful black velvet cape with a kind of Robin Hood hat and a large feather curling around his face. That cape was beautiful; I wanted it. Another was in an off-the-shoulder dress with a long shawl, and a third was a striking, tall boy whose tiny waist was encircled by a wide belt. In a group, they marched down to the front. The older black people sat with their faces frozen in shock. The young man with the belt pretended to be oblivious to the uproar. He was searching for a good seat. Out of his shoulder bag he took a lorgnette and used it to look around until he found the place he wanted. He took his seat, settled himself and—just as the church was starting to quiet down—looked up and saw me at the front. Fluttering his right hand in the air, he shouted, "Hiya, Shirley! Right on, gal!"

They were there because I had declared that homosexuals' civil rights had been infringed by society, and advocated that their equality with heterosexuals be supported by the laws. The Boston gay militants were only showing their approval, although I could have wished they were not camping it up quite so flagrantly. But I was delighted with the expressions on the audience's faces, and I gave the young man a cordial greeting. It did not end there; for the rest of the afternoon, as we went on to a rally outdoors near a large housing project, the gays appointed themselves my advance men; voters' mouths hung open as they were handed literature by men in drag who urged, "Vote for Shirley on Tuesday!" One boy, with lovely small blond curls, saw me arriving for the rally and seemed embarrassed. I went straight over to him and offered my hand. "I want to thank you for working for me," I said. He giggled nervously and shook my hand without a word. They stayed with me all the

Richard W. Johnson

At a rally sponsored by women's groups in Massachusetts
Mary Rosenfeld 1972

A greeting from a senior citizen in North Carolina, and a check for the campaign
Jim Stratford/Greensboro News & Record 1972

Along a parade route in Miami, Florida
Richard W. Johnson

A fund-raising party at home base—in Brooklyn
YMCA of Greater New York Public Relations Dept.

On "Meet the Press" with George McGovern, Hubert Humphrey, Edmund Muskie, and Henry Jackson
Bettmann/Getty Images

With Senator Henry Jackson and Senator Edmund Muskie
Source Unknown

With Senator Richard Newhouse in Chicago at a surprise birthday party
Bob Black/Chicago Sun-Times

way to the airport, where I caught a plane to New York late in the evening.

My speech, whether in English or Spanish, took the same line everywhere I stopped. "The other candidates," I would say, "are going to be coming in here, or their campaign workers are, and saying, 'Don't vote for Shirley Chisholm, because she has no chance to be President. Vote for somebody who can win.' Well, if I can't be President, I can be an instrument for change. Why do you think people are running around saying I can't be President? They know I have the intellect and creative ability to put it together. That's why they are afraid. They know that I can't be bought; they know I can't be bossed. They know I can't be controlled. I am asking my brothers and sisters to give me a chance. The time has come when we no longer have to be the passive recipients of whatever the politicians of this nation may decree for us. We no longer have to remain disillusioned, apathetic, helpless and powerless. We now have a person who is willing to accept the snubs, the snide remarks, the humiliation and abuses because she dares to go against the tradition in this country—a country in which only white males can run for the Presidency. I am willing, because I understand."

At the Elma Lewis School of Fine Arts in Roxbury, where about two hundred people were gathered, I expanded on the theme. "They have never sat down and asked black people what the ticket should look like, and blacks are 25 percent of the Democratic vote. And they certainly haven't asked women." All along Roxbury's black belt that afternoon, I pleaded with people not to let me down. But I heard one man in a blue Stetson tell a friend, "Vote? Shoot, I ain't no citizen. They're going to burn you up anyway when they get ready."

From Roxbury we drove to a cocktail party fund-raiser in Newton, where about three hundred Greater Bostonians, predominantly white, had met in a white-columned mansion with a center hall and staircase that looked like an antebellum Southern Big House. Alderman Matthew Jefferson of Newton predicted "great possibilities" for a Chisholm coalition in Massachusetts' Fourth Congressional District. Mark Solomon, like Jefferson a state delegate, said the Chisholm forces could have a "power broker role" at the Miami convention. "She is a dark horse in a gray field of white male candidates," Solomon said. "She's the only candidate I'd accept a kiss from."

Tuesday came, and with 22,398 votes I finished fifth in Massachusetts, behind McGovern, Muskie, Wallace and Humphrey. McGovern had a total vote of 325,673. But I had seven delegates and my state campaign coordinator, Jim Pitts, was one. He was elected to the Platform Committee. Saundra Graham, also a delegate, was put on the Credentials Committee.

Every office-seeker tries to nurture the illusion that his or her support has sprung up spontaneously from the grass roots, without having been sought. Over and over again in my campaign, I swear it really happened. Take

New Mexico, a state I had no thought of entering. A thirty-seven-year-old mother of five, Mrs. Tashia Young, phoned me one day during the late winter, after much trouble in getting through, to ask my permission to enter my name in the primary. I warned her that New Mexico wasn't one of the states in which I expected much support and that I would be unable to fit it into my crowded schedule. But she insisted that she and others wanted to have a real choice in the primary, and they only wanted my blessing. This woman had borrowed $500 to enter my name and had organizations going in Albuquerque, Las Cruces and Farmington. It was an amazing demonstration of courage and idealism. I have never met Mrs. Young to this day, but someday I hope to. Predictably, I did not get many votes in New Mexico, but that was not the fault of Mrs. Young and her small band of volunteers.

After Massachusetts, the next primary was North Carolina, where the Sanford camp was becoming afraid that I would deny a majority to the former governor and let Wallace win the state. This became their watchword: "A vote for Chisholm is a vote for Wallace." In traditional Southern style, they tried to play on local pride by making it a contest between North Carolina and Alabama, as if it were some kind of football game, and damn the national issues. My failure to spend much time in the state was seized upon; a television commentator in Winston-Salem speculated that I had really dropped out of the race. Newspapers friendly to Sanford, which most of the major ones were, gave prominence to any story that could be considered anti-Chisholm, such as an interview in Colorado in which something I said was interpreted as meaning that I favored Wallace. There was Florida-type trouble in my campaign organization—feuding between white women and young black men over who was calling the plays. As in Florida, the opposition, by which I mean Sanford supporters, not Wallace-ites, tried to make me out a stalking-horse.

"Stalking-horse" is one of those words and phrases that have gained a unique meaning in the United States because of their usefulness in politics. Others that come to mind are "mandate," meaning winning with anything over 51 percent, and "tantamount," meaning winning the primary where the other party is feeble, as in "tantamount to election." Apparently it used to be a ruse of hunters to creep up to game behind the concealment of a horse's body, on the theory that animals would not be frightened by another animal, as long as the hunter was out of sight. In politics, it has acquired a metaphorical meaning that, frankly, I cannot connect very well with the original significance of the phrase. It means a phony candidate, one who enters in order to split the vote and assist another entrant in the race. In Florida I was a stalking-horse for Lindsay, according to some of the experts. In North Carolina I was a stalking-horse for McGovern, according to one theory; my function was supposedly to keep Sanford from sewing up the delegation for delivery to Humphrey or Muskie. This is the kind of silliness that appeals to people who don't have much

experience in politics and to whose unformed judgments
intrigue is the same thing as strategy. It was perfectly clear
to anyone who knew the score that my entry in Florida,
North Carolina and everywhere else was, on the whole,
more damaging to the candidates I was supposed to be a
stalking-horse for than it was to their opponents.

What piqued me about the stalking-horse nonsense
was not its falsity to fact, because that is what one expects
from political reporting, a field in which the writers who
sound most authoritative are precisely those who have no
idea what is really going on. It was that it typified the basic
misconception about my candidacy, that it had some other
objective than winning the nomination for President. It was
another way of expressing the judgment "She must know
she can't win, so obviously she isn't serious." In this case it
was "She knows she can't win, so she must have some other
devious purpose." No one except the committed minority
who worked for me seemed able to grasp the fact that I always mean what I say; I was running for President to win.
Some analysts decided I was campaigning for the symbolic
value of having a black woman candidate in the field; it was
true that one of the values of my candidacy was the symbolic
one, but that was not the main point. Others said my real
goal was to collect enough votes to be in a position to deal
from strength at the convention; this was true too, as I made
clear repeatedly, but that was not all. Some, less kind, repeated that I was only "on an ego trip"; it is true that it takes
a good opinion of one's abilities to seriously offer oneself as

a candidate for the hardest job in the world, and I am not often charged with false modesty, either, but there are more satisfying ways of expressing one's self-esteem than going on a killing nine-month schedule of campaigning and going hundreds of thousands of dollars in debt.

Back to North Carolina. My big campaign tour there, as in earlier primaries, had to be concentrated on the weekend before the primary. It was the third, fourth and fifth of May, and it was in many ways a repeat of the experiences I had touring northern Florida. We visited small town after small town, places off the main roads, and I spoke to people from courthouse steps and in muddy fields. The response was unmistakable; there was a spirit there that had been completely underestimated among rural Southern blacks who were seeing something they had never dreamed of seeing, one of their sisters running for the Presidency of the United States. I begged them, as I had in Massachusetts, to support me instead of one of the white men who had fooled and then forgotten them through the years. "If Terry Sanford cares so much about stopping Wallace," I asked, "why doesn't he get out of the primary? After all, he's only a favorite son. I'm the national candidate here." In a place called Pembroke, a heavily Indian town, I broke into tears at seeing the Indians in the crowd; I had to fight to regain control of myself. It had suddenly come home to me that these people had been here for four hundred years, the victims of abuse and degradation at the hands of whites that was every bit as terrible and of even longer duration than blacks had suffered; I remembered something I had read by a western Indian chief who was telling about the starvation of the babies in his tribe: they looked, he said, "like rats." It was such a terrible image; I was overcome.

We got nearly 9 percent of the vote in North Carolina, a total of 61,723; Wallace carried the state with about 50 percent, Sanford got about 34 percent. I was third; Muskie had half as many votes as I did, and Jackson far fewer, less than 1 percent. But the state rule was that no candidate with less than 15 percent of the total got any delegates, so I had nothing to show for the primary in delegate totals. It was no cause for regret; the experience of campaigning through the poor towns of the black South and the strength and spirit of the people I met there made it well worthwhile. I would do it again tomorrow.

One of the surprising events of the campaign was that I picked up eight delegates from Hubert H. Humphrey's home state, Minnesota. I had several backers in the Democratic Farmer-Labor Party, a still-flourishing descendant of the Bob La Follette Progressives of several generations back. On a Wednesday evening in March I flew to Minneapolis–St. Paul and was met at Metropolitan Airport by three hundred supporters and Humphrey himself, who greeted me in effusive style for the photographers and television cameramen. It was an uproarious crowd; people kept pushing out of it to shake hands. "You've got spunk," one woman said, embracing me. (I wonder if any of the other candidates were hugged and kissed as much as I was?) There was a rally at Hamline University, with what must have been two thousand people in the auditorium. Keenly aware that blacks made up 3 percent or less of Minnesota's population, I pitched my appeal to all groups.

"Join with me on the Chisholm Trail! If you believe in my ability, intelligence and courage, you will join me! The blacks alone in America can't do it. The young people alone can't do it. The women alone can't do it. But together all these groups can rise up to get their share of the American dream and participate in the decision-making process that governs our lives. I have suffered; my people have suffered. Women have suffered; they have not been given access to the decision-making process. We need to be in the seat of power."

A program of student poetry readings and music by a black vocal group and the Hamline Jazz Lab band had warmed the audience up for a tumultuous ovation when my turn came; it was one of the biggest, most enthusiastic crowds I can remember addressing. As I looked out over them I could not help feeling that I was seeing the future of America as it should be, as it must be—black and white youth together, black and white adults, women, children, Indians, Hispano-Americans, the alienated and left-out joined with the mainstream of the nation at last, all reaching out to be included in the democratic process. It was a peak moment for me, and the exhilaration lasted through a meeting with the district convention delegates who were going to be committed to me, and persisted even until I boarded a plane back to Washington the next morning.

Michigan had the first Presidential primary in its history in 1972, on May 16, and the leading Democratic candidates pretty well conceded it in advance to Governor George C. Wallace. Once a liberal Democratic bastion, Michigan was divided by bitter emotions over court-ordered busing to desegregate schools in Detroit and other cities. For a black candidate to look for votes where the white liberals had abandoned hope seemed futile. But that was not the whole story. First, the very fact that the white candidates felt compelled to pussyfoot through this Wallace-country-north made it important for me to go in and give tongue to the issues that they were certain to gloss over. Second, even in the face of the anti-busing hysteria, support was sprouting for me. It was led by a slim young black woman pharmacist named Jacqui Hoop, who organized the main Chisholm for President headquarters in Ann Arbor and plunged into developing a statewide volunteer organization. Her energy and ingenuity inspired others, and headquarters opened in Flint, Kalamazoo, East Lansing, Detroit, Battle Creek and Inkster. The volunteers were almost equally divided between blacks and whites; their fervor in that apparently hopeless campaign was something to see. Some of the original silk-screened posters they turned out were the most beautiful I have ever seen in a political campaign. They put the same talent and extra effort into canvassing, taking my unlikely candidacy directly to thousands of homes. The opposition they encountered only inspired them to work harder, and their lack of money became one more exciting challenge. It had to be seen to be believed.

There was Ann Kirkwood of Ferndale, who told a newspaper reporter who asked why she was working for me, "I believe a woman's voice should be heard. I like the things Mrs. Chisholm has to say. . . . Her candidacy is one way to get persons to listen to what she has to say, and I think she might have some play in the convention, even though I believe it is too soon for a woman to be a Presidential candidate." A member of the League of Women Voters, she had never been active in partisan politics before. Another woman, Loletia Henson of Huntington Woods, a language teacher at the Orchard Ridge campus of Oakland Community College, was a candidate for precinct delegate. A newspaper quoted her: "I think she's the best candidate. I don't think she can win at this time, but I'd like to see her do well so she'll have an influence at the national convention."

There was a two-day swing across Michigan in late April, starting with a breakfast at the Grand Rapids YWCA, attended by League of Women Voters members, ministers' wives and other women. Women volunteers were so enthusiastic and conspicuous in the Michigan campaign that Jacqui Hoop and another Chisholm leader, Drew Sparks, had to keep making the point that the campaign was not aimed solely at women. From Grand Rapids we went to Kalamazoo and an enthusiastic audience of about one thousand whites and blacks, in Bronson Park. I bore down on civil rights and welfare, two of the most unpopular subjects in Michigan at that moment.

"We have all heard the tired rhetoric of politicians about the brotherhood of man, the American concept of democracy and equality of opportunity, and we have long noted that the politicians don't suit their actions to their words. Traditionally, the Presidency has been the exclusive domain of a sole segment of our society—white males. This says to the others in our multifaceted, multiracial society that they unfortunately don't have the leadership or the brainpower to lead. This is no time to be hung up on sex or race. In 1972, we Americans need the best collective abilities of all our people. We Americans need to lift the burdens of unfairness and discrimination from the shoulders of so many of our fellow countrymen, of both sexes, all ages, and all races. This is why I call for tax reform, to ensure that each man pays his fair share based on his income; that is why I call for welfare reform and a national system of day care centers, to minimize the number of families in the aid-to-dependent children (ADC) category of state social services budgets. And that is why I call for equal justice before the law, for young as well as old, black as well as white, and poor as well as rich. . . .

"Who knows? It took a little black woman, Harriet Tubman, to lead three hundred of her people out of slavery; it required another little black woman, Rosa Parks, to say she was tired of going to the back of the bus for a seat, and this act of very real courage precipitated the Montgomery bus boycott, which was a turning point in the civil rights struggle. It may take another little black woman to 'bring us together' in these troubled times of war and worry."

At Battle Creek, between a housing project dedication at which I spoke and a meeting with local Democratic officials, we made time to visit the grave of another black woman, not a little one but a giant physically as well as spiritually. I put a wreath on her grave and read the sign there: "Sojourner Truth, a renowned lecturer and reformer who championed anti-slavery, rights of women and the freedmen, rests here."

The Michigan campaign Jacqui Hoop, Drew Sparks and others like Nita Hardie of Battle Creek had laid out was a double-barreled one, professionally conceived and executed. The main goal was to get precinct delegates to run for me; this was a matter of personal contact. The second aim was publicity, to make me better known in communities across the state; this was a matter of getting news coverage, which in the atmosphere of those months in Michigan was not difficult. "We don't have enough money for an electronic media campaign," Jacqui told a reporter. "It's a person-to-person campaign, and in a way it's kind of fortunate that we can't afford all the radio and television time. It makes it a nicer, more personal campaign."

My presence in his state put pressure on Representative John Conyers of Detroit to take a stand on my candidacy. He solved the problem I posed for him with a novel stroke: in primaries where I was entered, he would support me, Conyers said, and in the rest he would support George McGovern. This kind of endorsement seemed to some of my supporters an attempt to enjoy the best of two worlds, but considering how many other politicians never saw fit to endorse me in any way in spite of offering all kinds of "encouragement," I suppose I should have been grateful even for this ambivalent stand.

The state Democratic chairman, James McNeely, called a strategy session to make plans to combat Governor Wallace. Representatives of Senators Edmund Muskie, George McGovern and Hubert Humphrey attended, but McNeely failed to invite any of my people. A spokesman said later it was "an oversight," an explanation almost as belittling as the original snub. We were not surprised; that kind of thing had happened repeatedly and was to happen again.

One prominent Michigan resident's generosity is something I will never forget. Jane Hart, wife of one of the most conscientious and distinguished Senators, Phil Hart, became an ardent moral and financial supporter. She loaned us her farm near Frederick, Maryland, for a fund-raising picnic, with entertainment, swimming, music, sports and dancing. Eugene McCarthy stopped by to see me, and the actor whose resemblance to the President is so astonishing that he has made a career of impersonating Nixon under the name of Richard M. Dixon also came and encouraged me to stay in the race.

Just before the Michigan primary, I made another three-day swing through the state. In Detroit I appeared at a peace and justice rally at Kennedy Square and at a meeting of about two thousand persons in the Detroit Hilton, sponsored by the Detroit Press Club. At a rally in Inkster, people huddled under umbrellas in a downpour waiting for me to arrive. On May 15, just after a brief stop at a community home for children, something shocking happened. A sheriff's deputy said he had just had a report that George Wallace had been shot in Maryland.

VIII.

Wallace's Shooting

"WE'RE ALL ANIMALS," I remember repeating, as we drove to the airport. We were scheduled to leave directly for San Francisco, but I was so shaken and confused that I decided, if it was someone black, I was going right back to New York. On the way, we heard a report (soon proved false) that several blacks had been arrested. If there ever was a moment when I was ready to withdraw from the campaign, this was it. If a black was the assassin, who knows what ugly retaliation against blacks might follow the shooting? Who would be the prime target but me?

At the airport, we learned more about what had happened, that it was a white man, apparently acting alone, and that Wallace was still alive. Roger Barr, my tireless white volunteer from Florida, was with me, dressed funkily as usual. The manager of the airport restaurant asked him to leave. Roger at that moment was on the phone with Representative Charles C. Diggs, Jr., of Detroit, taking down an endorsement from Diggs. "We always get endorsed the night before the primary," he told me angrily. Calming down a little, we conferred and decided to fly on to California. By coincidence, Senator McGovern was on the same plane; we did not talk to each other during the flight. Detroit reporters, we learned later, had rushed to the airport to catch me after they learned of Wallace's shooting and were angry when they found I had left before they arrived.

When we landed in San Francisco, a detachment of Secret Service agents was waiting for me. No protection had been provided for me until then because I had not reached 5 percent in the national polls, the criterion that somebody or other had decided on. But from then through the Miami convention, they were with me round the clock. As a matter of fact, the detachment of agents I was assigned became almost members of the family. They hit it off beautifully with Conrad, whose background as an investigator made them kindred souls. I was grateful for their presence and did everything I could to make their lives a little easier; when we were in Brooklyn, between trips, we fixed a room downstairs in our house with card tables and a television set for the men. I was astonished to learn that this was an unusual thing for a protectee to do; many candidates, they told me, made them stay outside, whatever the weather, and treated them as if they didn't exist. Some of my staff were told that before long the "Chisholm detail" became a prized assignment. Before they left me in Miami, the chief of the detachment, John Paul Jones, and his men gave me an unusual present that is one of my most treasured souvenirs of the campaign—a scrapbook with every day's itinerary during the weeks they were with me and pictures of all the agents who were assigned to me, meticulously mounted.

It was impossible for me not to think of the risk of being attacked, a danger that had occurred to me many times before. Most public figures attract a certain amount of hate mail; I had always received my share, most of it depressingly unimaginative in its obscenity and racial hatred. Many times, Conrad and I had felt certain someone was keeping watch on our house in Brooklyn; we had long since formed the habit of trying to lead our personal lives with a minimum of publicity, in order to reduce the risks of exposure to someone's pathological hatred that might find me a convenient outlet. That unforgettable year of 1968 in which Martin Luther King's killing was followed by that of Robert F. Kennedy was still fresh in everyone's memory. Was 1972 to be another, and if so, who would be the next victim? I could not afford to let hate mail and anonymous phone calls paralyze me; the risk had to be taken. The real tragedy would be to let the acts of a few deranged men disrupt the political life of the country; the loss of great leaders like Dr. King and the Kennedys was an incalculable one, but if the effect was to frighten any potentially controversial figure into seclusion and inactivity, the damage would be greater still.

The truth was that at no time during the campaign did I ever feel personally threatened by the crowds I was surrounded by: quite the reverse; they were all warm and receptive. But who could tell what hostility or racial hate was concealed behind one of those friendly-seeming faces?

Most of the time the possibility is only a faint, nagging thought below the level of conscious attention. But from time to time it surfaces. I could not help musing that the taking of a life was perhaps only an extreme manifestation of the kind of political incivility that had become our national style in recent years. Deep personal hatreds and vendettas have been flaunted at the highest levels. I recalled stories of the vicious White House attitudes toward those who opposed President Nixon, such as Representative Paul McCloskey and Senators Goodell, Gore and Fulbright. Congressional debates, particularly those on busing and home rule for the District of Columbia, have been so loaded with vitriolic and sickening hatred directed toward individuals and groups that I have left the floor of the House feeling physically upset. The decline of civility and the mounting crudeness of language in our public life could also be another reason for the disgust of people with politicians and government officials and the contempt manifested toward them. The consequences for public debate and the rational, civilized conduct of public affairs are grave. This collapse in communication is terribly sad. It is a steady tearing asunder of the few threads which bind us together in a society undergoing massive change. It is sad, too, that so many of our public personalities lack *size*, that tolerance and generosity that spring from self-confidence and goodwill.

When Governor Wallace was reported recovering and

able to receive visitors at Holy Cross Hospital in Silver Spring, Maryland, I went to pay him a call. No two candidates, perhaps no two people, could differ more vehemently on many of the issues of public policy, but I could not see that this ought to have any relationship to our private behavior toward each other. With one of my Congressional staff aides and several Secret Service men, I drove out and spent twenty minutes with him. Governor Wallace seemed sincerely touched. He cried for a moment, and so did I. "Is that really you, Shirley?" he asked. "Have you come to see me?" What we talked about was nothing earthshaking; it was like almost any other sick call. I did say at one point, "You and I don't agree, but you've been shot, and I might be shot, and we are both the children of American democracy, so I wanted to come and see you."

The press was waiting outside when I emerged. I had not told anyone I was going, and I was surprised to find them there, but I suppose they were keeping a watch on the hospital to see who came and went. My visit to Wallace may have had more press attention than anything else I did during the campaign, and more, it seemed, than the calls a number of other people paid on the wounded Alabama governor. It seemed to me that the excessive attention paid to what I intended to be a simple, private expression of human sympathy and concern was, in another way, a revelation of the same sickness in public life that leads to assassinations. Why should my visit be considered so colorful and newsworthy? Had politics, or race relations, reached such a point that it was to be thought of as bizarre? Naturally, some people began at once to speculate on my political motives for the visit. Why were they compelled to look for any? Was it so strange that my motive was only common decency and courtesy? There were black politicians who insinuated that some kind of a deal was being cooked up! One black man from Texas, a delegate pledged to me, was so angry that he threatened to withdraw his support. What hurdles we Americans must still have to clear as we grope our way toward a civilized society, when such a simple gesture is deemed newsworthy and a sign of political intrigue!

During the campaign there was a poster on sale in novelty stores that showed Governor Wallace and me in the famous pose of the painting "American Gothic." I never quite got the point, if it had one, and I hope it was withdrawn from the market after the Governor's tragic injury. But it was true that there was a parallel between George Wallace's candidacy and mine, and there were places—such as northern Florida and North Carolina—where we seemed to be the only two candidates in the field. Although we represented opposite poles on many questions of policy, we both spoke for groups who felt dispossessed by the establishment and alienated by the course our society is taking. As I noted earlier, Wallace said of me approvingly, more than once, "She's the only other one who says the same things in Florida that she says in Washington," meaning thereby to indict his other primary opponents for what we might delicately term inconsistency. Many people were supporting

Wallace because he talked about issues that were important to them—the unresponsiveness of the government to the people, the unfairness of the tax structure and dominance of huge corporate institutions. These were also basic themes in my campaign. To that extent, we were both political mavericks and both "people's" candidates. There, of course, the similarity ended. But I learned during the campaign that not all Wallace supporters were racists; there are many decent, average individuals in America who have been abandoned by "politics as usual" and relegated to powerless positions, and who have found what they believe to be a spokesman for their cause in George Wallace. There are, I am sad to say, many bigots who are Wallace-ites, and this is because some of the views he upholds are those agreeable to racists. I am fiercely opposed to some of his positions; for instance, I support school busing as a means, limited and makeshift though it may be, to start correcting the effects of race prejudice and segregated housing patterns, on equality of educational opportunity. But belief in the right of another to hold and publicly advocate the contrary point of view without having his motives impugned and his character maligned seems to me to be a fundamental tenet of our political system. This tolerance and mutual respect is fundamental to democracy's survival.

IX.

The Last Primary

As PREDICTED, I was crushed in Michigan. The great response I thought I had felt did not express itself in votes. George Wallace walked off with a solid majority of the state, and most of the votes I had been hoping for were split between McGovern and Humphrey. Perhaps it was that people who sympathized with me still considered that they would be wasting their votes on me; politics in this country is a game that most people feel should be played to win, and it was hard for me to persuade them to use their votes to "shake up the system within the system," as I kept urging.

When the returns came in, I was in California on a final campaign trip through a state I had originally intended to avoid. The only chance that I could get any delegates in California rested on a challenge to the state's retention of the old winner-take-all system, under a special exception to the reform rules written by the McGovern Commission. Hubert H. Humphrey, whose fading hopes could be revived only by winning in California, had filed a lawsuit to have the exception thrown out. Senator Henry M. Jackson of Washington joined the action, and at Humphrey's invitation so did I. This got me labeled as part of the stop-McGovern coalition. From the point of view of a McGovern backer, I suppose that was true. But my motive was never to stop McGovern, or to aid Humphrey or anyone else except myself. If I was entitled to any votes from California, I wanted them; I was a candidate myself, as I kept trying to make other politicians remember. To have votes for me count for nothing seemed just plain wrong, and still seems that way. It was not McGovern I opposed, but the winner-take-all rule. One candidate in a field of four or five could get all the delegates with a plurality of less than 50 percent. Who, then, represents the majority of the voters who wanted other candidates? While the McGovern Commission held its hearings, I took the position that the winner-take-all system was wrong, and I have maintained that view ever since. If anyone failed to realize that I was upholding a view I had always held, not simply arguing against winner-take-all for personal advantage, it had to be that they had paid no attention to my views. As usual, they may have felt what I thought was not important.

It was not in the slim hope of getting some delegate votes that I went to California, but in order not to disappoint some of the most enthusiastic supporters I had anywhere. At Ron Dellums' invitation I had been in the San Francisco Bay Area as early as October, 1971, and found women's groups, in particular, anxious for me to enter. Members of the Berkeley chapter of the National Organization for Women (NOW) had already endorsed me, and so had several leaders of the California Women's Political Caucus and the northern California women's division of the Democratic Party. There were also local groups called Women Organized for Political Action and Women for Peace announcing their support. In Venice there was even a Republicans for Chisholm group. By early 1972 there were also a number of Los Angeles area residents pressing me to come into California, and my mail kept bringing contributions and offers of support from all parts of the state—Sacramento, San Bernardino, San Diego. It was not possible to accept it all; we had no money to run a campaign in California. My slim resources were not adequate for the East Coast and Midwest primaries I was in; I tried to make it clear to the Californians that, since they were so enthusiastic, I could not refuse to enter the primary, but all the organizing would have to be done by volunteers. My national campaign office could not send any money, and I would not be responsible for any debt in California. All I could do was come out for a few campaign tours. This approach puzzled some potential supporters, and alienated some. They could not understand why their offers of help were not answered with assistance and instructions; they felt rejected and decided that I was not grateful for their backing and I was not serious about running in California.

In March I even started getting phone calls from San Francisco and Los Angeles wanting to know whether I was campaigning in California or not; the uncertainty was especially great after I canceled an appearance at a Concerned Democrats of California convention. My Bay Area supporters had been counting on having me come to this left-liberal Democratic group's meeting to make an appeal for support, and they had planned to have a motorcade and a round of other events at the same time. But I had just wound up the Florida primary, and fatigue had helped bring on an attack of laryngitis. My doctor ordered me to bed and forbade me even to speak to the meeting by long-distance telephone through a loudspeaker. My absence naturally dimmed the enthusiasm of some of my backers.

The group dynamics involved in my California campaign organization, from the descriptions I heard during and after the campaign, would make a fascinating study for some psychologist or sociologist. The rivalry between black men and white women campaign workers, which was troublesome in Florida, North Carolina and other states, became bitter hostility there. There was a class at Mills College in Oakland, called "Candidates, Campaigns and Constituents," taught by Dr. Frances Mullins, and it was apparently intended to be a real experience in practical politics; the students organized into groups to work for the candidates they supported in the primary campaign from February through May. There was a Chisholm group that included what were to be some of my hardest-working supporters in Berkeley and Oakland. I have a folder of the papers they wrote at the end of the course, and several of them tell vividly how the black male/white female disputes developed. "Although they may have intellectually understood the parallels between racial and sexual discrimination," one says, "many of the black men involved in the East Bay Steering Committee found it difficult to identify with women's oppression." For instance, one young black could not understand why a white woman student was angry when he did not want to help clean up an office for its grand opening. Another man told Judy Bertelson, a Mills College faculty member who was working for me, that she had a petty concern with details, "common to women."

The best-organized faction in the campaign, both in the Bay Area and in Los Angeles, seems to have been the NOW women. They were the motive force in the early part of the campaign, organizing meetings and circulating petitions to put my name on the ballot. "This in time," Dr. Frances Mullins wrote in a short review of my campaign as she and her class saw it, "created its own problems, because the NOW women became increasingly independent and separate from the other groups in the campaign." Just as the blacks often offended the women by accident, the women estranged blacks by lack of understanding, it appears. There was an important canvassing rally in Berkeley; no blacks were there. The climax of the problems caused by lack of communication and cooperation came when the NOW group changed the route for the projected motorcade (the one I never rode in) on the eve of the Concerned Democrats' convention. To ease my crowded schedule for the afternoon, they cut out the Hunter's Point area, which is heavily black, and they made the change without contacting black representatives in the campaign. There were cries that the women had taken over and were freezing out the poor and the black.

The same kind of disagreements plagued the Los Angeles area, where my southern California campaign coordinator, Arlie Scott, a University of Southern California history professor, did a vigorous and capable organizing job, only to provoke a barrage of criticism from blacks who said she and the other white women were dominating the whole scene. Some, I am told, were even threatened physically. Part of the trouble was that I and my handful of campaign workers in Washington steadfastly refused to call the shots and pick the leaders. As Dr. Mullins analyzed it, the effect was to sharpen conflicts between groups. In a more traditional campaign, she wrote in her post-mortem, the professional managers act as mediators between groups, keeping them separate and preventing direct clashes.

"Typically," she explained, "only the political elite representatives of these groups come together in major parties' conferences and conventions. By virtue of their political experience, they are expected to understand the value of compromise to preserve the coalition." But in the Chisholm group, by contrast, the first problem was to build an organization from the inexperienced volunteers, and then to select leaders. This meant that all the volunteers were in contact with each other from the beginning, and the result was a direct power struggle. The factions became sharply defined and hostile to each other. The demands of each interest group became involved with the question of selecting leaders, and long meetings were held over a period of two months. During this time-consuming process, many volunteers lost their desire to work, feeling they did not have energy for the intense, prolonged, complicated confrontation that took place at each meeting. They wanted me to solve the problem by appointing a leader for them. It took some time for them to understand that I was not going to do this. In the end, the leaders of both of the main factions in the Bay Area—the young black men and the NOW women—dropped out, and a new coordinator for the northern campaign was agreed on, Wilson Riles, Jr. Two of the Mills College students, Barbara Lee and Sandra Gaines, emerged in leadership posts. Both are welfare mothers in their twenties; they have two and three children respectively, and were juniors at the time of the campaign. With their relative maturity and broader background—roots in the black community and experience in the world of the NOW women—they were able to mediate between the two groups and provide the unifying leadership that was needed.

Dr. Mullins' study of the campaign makes a very interesting and important observation about these women and their emergence as leaders in the group, and it is the reason I have told the story fairly fully. Both were inexperienced in politics; Barbara had never even registered to vote before. But in the end they were to be responsible for a 9.6 percent vote for me in Alameda County. "They stand as a tribute that this grass-roots campaign was able to bring forth truly effective and representative leaders," Dr. Mullins said. The process was difficult and time-consuming; if it had not started early it could still have been going on when primary day came. But it worked. They were leaders who had been democratically selected and had the respect and commitment of the group; they could operate without having the aura of power and authority that an outside leader would have relied on; they led by keeping the group informed and involved in the decisions. The realization that the democratic process had proved itself effective after all restored, Dr. Mullins said, the idealism with which the campaign had begun. The participants in the experience realized that "democracy must be part of the means as well as the end of a democratic campaign." The conflict between women and blacks in my campaign would be, as I said, a worthwhile study for some sociologists. That it resulted, in the Bay Area, in an effective coalition shows that there can be successful resolutions of this kind of difficulty. In other areas, the same problem was not solved, but it could have been if the participants had persisted in the effort to work together long enough to survive the necessary stage of competition for dominance.

There is a great deal of naïveté about politics among both women and blacks, for the natural reason that neither group has taken much part in politics until recently. Women particularly are having difficulty in learning how much give and take are necessary. The women who worked for McGovern were crushed when he failed to support an abortion plank in his platform; they thought they had his allegiance on the issue and could not believe it when his staff maneuvered to let an abortion-on-demand plank be defeated. They could not accept the political necessity of compromising on the issue for the sake of other gains. Political beginners always seem to lay down elaborate programs and refuse to compromise on any detail of them. Blacks do it, and so do most other special-interest groups new to politics. In time, they learn to surrender in one place to win in another; they learn to bide their time and build support where it is weak.

For me, the conflict between blacks and white women appeared to be a competition over which group was going to own me and my candidacy, and I was determined to keep from becoming the captive of either. Militant blacks would challenge me at meetings and rallies to get those white women out of the campaign and prove that I was black. Each time, I refused and explained the basic fact that it would take women *and* blacks *and* whites and others to elect a President. The idea of blackness has no place in national politics in the United States, I would say; this cost me support from people who were convinced I was selling out my race. Even if I had rejected the support of white women, which would have been wrong and undemocratic, I would probably not have picked up much black support for it. The criticism came from believers in separatism, and that is not my philosophical or political position.

One militant black group, however, endorsed me

strongly—the Black Panthers. National chairman Bobby Seale said I was "the best social critic of America's injustices to run for President from whatever party," and promised that the Panthers' full membership would work for me. More than one supporter wanted me to disavow the Panthers' endorsement, but I flatly refused. "The Black Panthers are citizens of the United States and they have a right to endorse whomever they decide to endorse," I told reporters in Sacramento, where we got word of the action. "What has happened to them as an oppressed group in America has led them to the conclusion that perhaps with me there is hope." From where I stood, it was a highly hopeful sign that this group appeared to be emerging into an active participation in elective politics; they were acting according to a principle that I had always strictly maintained: that the way to change the system must be to work within the system. To disavow their support would have been arrogant and inconsistent with my strongest principles; if failing to do so cost me any votes from whites and moderate blacks, so be it. They are my brothers and sisters too, and I was pleased and proud at their action. One thing that gratified me was that the Panthers had succeeded in rising above sex prejudice, something that many blacks find difficult; they were supporting me because of my positions and my programs, without regard to my being female. This showed that in some ways they were farther along the path of political maturity than some of the moderate leaders of elements of the black community, who, I am convinced, never took me seriously as a candidate because they were not capable of taking any woman seriously as a potential leader.

To speak for a moment in a wider context than that of my California campaign organization, it has been generally true that the women's movement has been a white middle-class phenomenon; black women share many of the same concerns as white ones, including the need for a national day care system and a guarantee of equal pay for equal work, but they have different priorities from white women. Blacks are still concerned with survival, while whites can afford the luxury of being concerned with improvement. Black men need a supportive attitude from their women; they can be easily angered by any suggestion that they are being domi-nated or led by females. This shows an insecurity, of course, but the cure for that is not to condemn them, but to help them overcome it by achieving success and attaining per-sonal security. Hence, many black women submerge their own talents in order not to outshine men.

Being concerned with survival, black women generally feel that some of the things white women in the feminist movement do are trivial—picketing men-only bars, sitting in at magazine offices, insisting on the title Ms. and the word "chairperson." But white and black women could work to-gether on economic issues, like job discrimination, where their needs are the same. The women's movement, generally speaking, has not made such issues paramount. The abor-tion question is also a divisive one; white women are stron-ger supporters of abortion on demand than black women, although most black women favor unrestricted abortions. As one put it to me once, "I just wish white women would get as concerned about the health and well-being of the black babies who are born, as they are about me being able not to have babies."

Some "liberated" women tend to be hostile to values which are important to blacks, for example, religion. Middle-class whites tend to approach the question of work from the point of view that it is a way to relieve the boredom of housework. For most black women, work is an economic necessity; they would love to be able to stay home in the appliance-equipped suburban houses that white women are fleeing from. Differences of lifestyle and of priorities will continue to make cooperation between white and black women difficult until the white-dominated movement understands the problem and makes a determined, sincere effort to change itself in the requisite ways.

To return to the California campaign, it was in this last primary that the McGovern forces took off the gloves where I was concerned. I do not mean that the Senator himself made any public attacks on me, or that any of his prominent supporters did. But a whispering campaign raged. "Chisholm can't possibly win. She's in California to help Humphrey beat George. All she wants to do is kill McGovern's chances. Don't waste your vote on her." That kind of talk was suddenly everywhere, my supporters found. It was far more intense than the similar campaign I had encountered in North Carolina. And there was much more bad feeling behind the tactic in California; my people told me that emotions were running high and that the McGovern supporters were really becoming bitter. They were incapable of seeing opposition to the Senator as anything other than a conspiracy. The man who had to take more of the heat on it than I did was Ron Dellums, who was caught in the middle. His reelection to the House in the fall depended to a significant extent on the support—financial and political—of a number of white voters in his Congressional District who were all-out McGovern backers. The pressure on him to endorse McGovern was all but unbearable, I have been told. He withstood it until the weekend before the convention. Black McGovern supporters were also working on him; one of the most prominent was Assemblyman Willie Brown, whose campaign to deliver the black vote to McGovern could not have been helped by the way Dellums stuck with me. It was hard for blacks to fight me too openly; I was the only black candidate, the only candidate who was, for instance, calling for Angela Davis' release on bail, and pounding away at issues important to blacks. Not to back me could be uncomfortable for them, but backing me would have carried drawbacks, too; they would not have been supporting the winner, and this is the worst mistake a politician can make. There is no advantage in having been right in a losing cause; progress, power and prerogatives come to the supporters of the candidate who wins.

McGovern won California with 1,550,000 votes to 1,375,000 for Humphrey. I was a distant third, with 157,435, enough to entitle me to twelve delegates if the primary votes were apportioned according to the totals. Whether this was to happen depended on the Democratic Credentials Committee, which would hear what McGovernites called "the California challenge" at a meeting in Washington the week before the July convention.

After more than six months of campaigning in eleven primaries, and leaving the California votes out of the reckoning, I had twenty-eight delegates.

There was little more I could do until the convention met on July 10, a month away. There was still a chance that McGovern would not win on the first ballot and it would develop into the kind of situation in which a black caucus of delegates could join with uncommitted women, Hispano-Americans and others to make their voices heard. The likelihood was that this would not happen, and that commitments to one of the white candidates would come ahead of concern for black needs, women's issues and so on. But there was always a chance that this would be the year of change and that I could play a part in the new politics at the convention.

X

The Convention

WE TOOK AN 11:00 p.m. flight from New York to Miami on the Saturday night before the convention, July 8. My party was small: two aides, Conrad, and eleven Secret Service men. The other passengers appeared to be bound for the convention, too; there was an excitement in the air aboard the plane. Some of the passengers shook hands and wished me good luck. One said, "Things aren't going to be the same in this country after you're nominated." "I hope not," I said. At Miami International Airport, there was a small crowd of reporters, photographers and supporters to greet me. The Secret Service formed a phalanx and forced past them all; without a speech and with hardly a word to the reporters, I was in a car and we were off for Miami Beach with motorcycles all around us, flashing their red lights. It was a lot more than I was used to, and I remember thinking this must be what it is like all the time when you're a president, or a queen. When we pulled up to the Deauville Hotel, there was a huge crowd on the steps, with hastily made placards. The hotel had refused to let us put up signs anywhere, as the other candidates had done at their headquarters hotels (many of them had huge billboards on the marquees). The crowd's enthusiasm was far greater than I had expected, especially in the middle of the night. I felt a convention air of unreality and abandon. The Secret Service men would not let me out of the car until a path had been cleared through the people who had surged into the driveway to surround us. I had to sit there for what seemed like half an hour. When the car doors finally opened, the crowd cheered, "Right on!" "We love you!" "Give 'em hell!" "Don't sell us out now!" A woman touched me and began shouting, "I touched her!"

They let me pass into the hotel lobby and crowded in behind me shouting, "Speech, Shirley! Speech!" At the foot of the stairs to the mezzanine stood Mayor Kenneth Gibson of Newark. Although a McGovern supporter, he had agreed to appear and greet me when he learned from one of my staff that no other prominent blacks were going to be there for my arrival, and he made a short but extremely warm speech welcoming me to Miami and the convention. I stood at the foot of the stairs and gave my standard campaign speech to the excited crowd. Then we went upstairs, my head already full of what I would say to the black delegate caucus meeting the next afternoon.

A fresh blow had been struck against the hope of black unity about two weeks before the convention. District of Columbia delegate Walter Fauntroy and Representatives

Louis Stokes and William Clay had made a move on June 26 that, if it had succeeded, would have put the nomination in McGovern's pocket by handing him a package of 96 uncommitted delegates, for which Fauntroy, Stokes and Clay would get the credit. They called a Washington press conference to announce that they had the votes pledged to McGovern and that he was over the top. They said McGovern in return had endorsed the program of the Gary, Indiana, National Black Political Convention, with two reservations—he would not go along with the stand the convention had taken against Israel, and he could not agree that busing for desegregation should be abolished. Superficially, it was the same strategy black leaders had been groping toward for a year, to put together a bloc of votes that would make the difference between nomination and defeat and use it as a lever to extract commitments from one of the white candidates. But it was not what it seemed. First, the commitment they seemed to have was in generalities and represented no new pledges from McGovern, nothing really different from the statement he had made months before that he could support the program proposed by the Congressional Black Caucus in mid-1971. Second, and at least equally serious, the action had not been one in which any representative group of black delegates or their leaders had had a part. In fact, when Fauntroy, Stokes and Clay released a list showing where their 96 delegates were coming from, a few hours' telephoning by Thaddeus Garrett of my staff and Arnold Pinkney of Humphrey's organization were all that was needed to prove that almost half of the 96 delegates Fauntroy claimed to have pledged to Mc-Govern had never pledged their votes to anybody or even been consulted. Many of them, in fact, were irate to learn that someone they did not know and had never even talked to was claiming to speak for them.

One of the angriest was Dr. Aaron Henry, chairman of the Democratic Party of the state of Mississippi. For him the issue was crucial. The Fauntroy-Clay-Stokes statement was made less than twenty-four hours before Henry was to appear to contest a credentials challenge to his delegation by Governor William Waller of Mississippi. Henry was confident of winning—but to do so he needed the support of Credentials Committee members who were backers of candidates other than McGovern. The report that his delegation was no longer uncommitted was not only false, it was potentially very damaging. Aaron was also irritated at the implication that he would or could "deliver" the votes of his delegates. He made strong public denials that any of his people had switched to McGovern; they were going to the convention uncommitted, just as they had planned for months, and it was his belief that Fauntroy and the others had sold out black interests for their own personal prestige and gain. (It was well known, although apparently not to Fauntroy, that Henry was a strong Chisholm sympathizer personally; his uncommitted stance was forced on him by the political situation.)

Among the votes that Fauntroy had "delivered" to Mc-Govern was his own District of Columbia delegation, the same votes that he had promised me he would hold back and release to me on the second ballot if I would stay out of the District primary.

There were 452 black delegates and alternates at Miami, and a majority were already committed. Most of them were McGovern delegates. About 90 were Humphrey's. When the black delegate caucus met, it would be a pointless debating contest, as things were shaping up. What would be the use of going through the motions of agreeing on a program and trying to get unified support for it, when something close to half the black delegates were already delivered to McGovern? The only chance that the black caucus would have a meaningful role to play was if McGovern lost the "California challenge." The party Credentials Committee had ruled that McGovern was not entitled to all of California's 271 delegates and ordered 151 of them to be distributed to Hubert Humphrey and other candidates, with 106 of them to Humphrey, 12 to me, and the rest to George Wallace, Edmund Muskie and Sam Yorty. But the full convention would vote on the question Monday night, and if McGovern won then, he was sure of nomination on the first ballot. There would be no need for him to pay any more than a polite acknowledgment to the black caucus.

There was only one chance left to change the script, and it was an unlikely one. If the black delegates could be roused to a sense of their potential strength and the historic opportunity it offered, and united for the early ballots, it would have to be by a personal appeal from me. Maybe I could get something going at the black caucus. In the superheated emotional atmosphere of a convention, people might be stirred into doing the unexpected; I had heard of such things happening. But for more than ten months black leaders had been working, often at cross-purposes, true, but working to solidify the black vote into a bloc; if this collective effort had failed, how could a mere passionate appeal from me do the job? It would be hard to make many of the delegates believe that anything but vanity and ambition were my motives. But what else was there to do? Maybe if I told them how and why I had been campaigning, and warned them of the perils of the course they were following, they would rally to my side.

I slept little that night, and was up at seven o'clock. The black caucus was scheduled at noon, but it did not get started until around 2:00 P.M. All the candidates were invited, and I was put first on the list. The way the room erupted into cheers and shouts when I came in gave me a thrill of hope. It took five minutes for the roar to die down. Individuals shouted to me through the noise, "Tell us the truth, sister!" "They're selling us out again!" "Tell it like it is!" When the hubbub had nearly quieted, one voice showed that the approval was not unanimous. "Get her out of here!" a man demanded. There was a fresh uproar as he was shouted down.

"Brothers and sisters!" I shouted in a voice made husky by the cold blast of the hotel air conditioning. "Think! You didn't come here to be delivered! Don't play yourselves cheap! You paid your own way here, and you worked hard to do it. A black boss is as bad as a white boss, and some black leaders are willing to advance their own political fortunes at the expense of the masses. Please! Think of yourselves!"

White politicians had bought and paid for their votes, I said; black bosses had been bought like sacks of potatoes. These modern Benedict Arnolds had already made the decisions, and they were the helpless pawns. But they did not have to follow such leaders, I said. "Go with me on the first ballot!" I pleaded. "And if you can't go with me, go uncommitted! Black people all over this country are watching what we do here!" The younger and more militant delegates cheered and cheered. But as I left, I could feel that nothing had changed. Perhaps a few more of the black delegates understood what had happened to them. Some of them told me later that, for the first time since coming to Miami, they saw what was going on.

McGovern followed me, and his appeal was to support him on the California challenge. Humphrey came in, to much cheering by older black delegates. He told them of his civil rights record dating back to 1948, when he pushed for equal representation and set off a white Southern walkout from a Democratic convention. The younger delegates gave him only polite applause. One young man told a reporter later, "We're not interested in background."

Willie Brown got up to echo McGovern's plea, "Give me back my delegation!," and move that the black caucus vote against the California challenge. But the motion was tabled. The caucus was too split to take any action, on California or on a candidate, although a long, noisy session went on until evening and resumed on Monday.

My northern California campaign coordinator, Wilson Riles, Jr., a University of Southern California student who is the son of the California superintendent of public education, said later he had the feeling that the black delegates were being put on the block and auctioned off. McGovern's appeal was dictated only by his need to win the California challenge and was like a bid at a slave auction, as he saw it. My delegates wanted to know how I wanted them to vote on California and several other issues, including abortion and a challenge to the under-representation of women from South Carolina. "Vote your consciences," I said over and over. "Vote your consciences." We put out a brief fact sheet giving my views on each of the platform issues and on the California challenge, but we stressed that these were only my opinions, and everyone should vote as he or she thought best.

The challenges would be settled at the first convention session Monday night. The platform would be adopted Tuesday, and the nominations were to be Wednesday night. Time was short and any maneuvering had to be fast. We played relatively little part in it. Thadd Garrett and Sherry Friedman, a fundraiser for my campaign and director of the Washington office of the Mississippi Democratic Party, were out trying to find uncommitted black delegates for me, especially in Southern delegations. They scored some successes. Thadd swung some votes in his home state delegation of Ohio, which wound up giving me 23. Jackie Parker, a Louisiana native who works on the staff of Representative James A. Burke of Massachusetts, had been working on Louisiana delegates in my behalf for some time; she redoubled her efforts, and we got 21 from her state. From the Mississippi delegation we were counting on 12, from Pennsylvania 9 more. Two Florida delegates switched to me, risking arrest because under the state's winner-take-all law they were obligated to vote for George Wallace.

But the main action centered on Hubert Humphrey, who was making a last-ditch effort to stop a McGovern victory on the first ballot. If he could not do it, no one else could. Before long, the Humphrey camp was convinced that there were no more delegates open to persuasion by the Minnesotan. Numbers of the uncommitted delegates and of those pledged to Muskie, Jackson and others were going to vote against the California challenge. Humphrey was finished if the challenge failed. And it did fail. The convention voted by a safe margin to expel the Humphrey, Chisholm, Wallace, Muskie and Yorty delegates from California and replace them with McGovern supporters.

McGovern had his delegates back, and there was no way he could be denied the nomination. Muskie and Jackson withdrew. Then Humphrey released his delegates and suggested that about 90 black delegates who had been pledged to him support me. This was a move that Thadd Garrett had been working for. Arnold Pinkney, Humphrey's chief black lieutenant, was from Thadd's home state of Ohio and they had kept in touch during the campaign, working together at one point to refute Fauntroy's claim that he had lined up enough black delegates to clinch a victory for McGovern. Now they proposed to Humphrey that he try to throw his votes to me. Announcement of the action brought angry complaints from black McGovern supporters. They said Humphrey was trying to use me in a final desperate effort to block McGovern.

No doubt that was how it looked from the upper floors of the Doral Hotel, where the McGovern campaign staff was based. In their minds I had always been only a tool of Humphrey. Julian Bond had used the charge in caucuses where he was trying to win over unpledged delegates. He and Sherry Friedman had faced off on this in a Mississippi black caucus. Sherry's argument was that it was wrong to conclude that since Hubert Humphrey opposed winner-take-all in California and Shirley Chisholm did, too, hence they were allies; McGovern himself had been against winner-take-all in 1971. How could it have been wrong in 1971 and right in 1972? Bond's male chauvinism, Sherry told us later, was keeping him from believing that anyone could really be for me; he could not understand that and assumed that they were really for Humphrey and were using me as some kind of a decoy. In the end we got 12 of Mississippi's 25 votes.

From where we sat, in two small suites at the Deauville Hotel, it was very simple. The Humphrey delegates were a badly needed windfall, and we were not going to turn them down for any reason, certainly not because it displeased the McGovernites. If Humphrey was playing some kind of deep game by releasing his delegates, we didn't mind, and there was no reason we could see to think this was what he was doing. Even with all 90 Humphrey delegates, we were not going to be in a position to prolong the voting to a second ballot, unless a lot more support appeared from out of the blue. Charles Evers, the mayor of Fayette, Mississippi, was working to swing black votes to me on the first ballot. He was trying to get all the other candidates to follow Humphrey's lead, and thus put pressure on McGovern. If McGovern insisted on withholding his black votes from me, he would look like a racist, the theory went; if he released them (an impossible eventuality), he would not have a majority on the first round. Senator Henry Jackson said his delegates were free to vote for me, when he withdrew. In the tension and uncertainty of the convention milieu, tempers flared. Jesse Jackson and other McGovern backers said the anti-McGovern forces were practicing conspiracy and racism. Representative Clay told the press, "I don't question Mrs. Chisholm's integrity, but I do question her judgment and at times her sanity." Suspicious of each other as much as they were of me, the black leaders jostled and competed for the television limelight. Walter Fauntroy had rumbles of defections in his own delegation. He, Stokes and Clay were scrambling to get and hold the votes they thought they were going to have neatly packaged for McGovern. The threat—hollow as it turned out to have been—was that a movement was developing toward me. To have his plan come apart at the eleventh hour would have been too humiliating. Fauntroy pleaded with blacks to consider what four more years of the Nixon administration would mean to them. Blacks must move to the center of the Democratic Party to act as a buffer between party regulars and the McGovernites, to heal the split left by the withdrawal of Muskie and Humphrey, he told an interviewer. They have to do this because it is they that have the most to lose; white youth and the party regulars can survive another term of Nixon, but blacks would suffer far more. McGovern "understood the need to unite the various factions," and Fauntroy's assignment was to help him do it.

One tactic the McGovern people used to hold delegates in line was as unappealing as it was persuasive. Delegates were told that they were legally bound to vote for the candidate they ran pledged to and faced jail sentences if they did not do so. Many came to a caucus of Chisholm delegates on Wednesday morning, the day of the balloting for the nomination, in an intense state of agitation. "If I vote for you, I'm going to get arrested when I step off the plane back home," they cried. Sherry Friedman told them that was not true, because their states' jurisdictions did not cover what they did in Florida, so the only delegates risking legal action were those from Florida. Anyway, Sherry said, "Going to jail is not so bad. Some things are important enough to go to jail for. If you're too weak to risk it, get out of here now." Aaron Henry and Mississippi state representative Kenneth Clark made similar speeches, and the one hundred or so delegates at the caucus left feeling better. For that matter, so did I; their fears had begun to unsettle me.

The night before the nomination, unexpected feelers came

from the Florida delegation, which was not only pledged to Wallace but overwhelmingly in favor of him. Some Floridians, through Aaron Henry, met with Sherry Friedman and in a cloak-and-dagger atmosphere confided that if the convention went to a second ballot, there were between 68 and 70 votes in Florida that were ready to shift to me, provided the delegation was polled in secret. Even if the balloting were open, I could count on 43 votes, we were told.

On the same night, many of the McGovern black leaders decided that they should get a solid endorsement for their candidate from the black delegate caucus. A meeting was hastily called, and Thadd Garrett went to represent me. But he had not been warned that the subject of the meeting was a McGovern endorsement and was thunderstruck when he arrived to learn that the chief black operatives for the two candidates—Fauntroy for McGovern and Thadd for me— were to make final arguments before the caucus voted on an endorsement. It was intended to be a coup d'état, and Fauntroy was confident that it would succeed. But Thadd recovered from his surprise and hit back in a speech that challenged Fauntroy to produce a list of the specific commitments to black needs that he was claiming McGovern had made. Fauntroy could not; the best he could manage was to call on the delegates to have faith and confidence in the people who were their "bargainers," and said weakly that he could not reveal all that had been promised. The delegates, even some already committed to McGovern, started questioning him and the other McGovern people more closely. Soon there were shouts of "Vote!" and something happened that I had never expected. The black caucus rejected McGovern completely and voted to endorse me, just hours before the nomination.

After the Monday night convention vote that "gave Mc-Govern his delegation back," it had seemed that the black unity drive was effectively over. For me to have taken an active role in further efforts to get the black delegates together would, it seemed to me, have magnified confusion, tensions and hostility to no good purpose. Some of my staff did not agree, and I had made no effort to keep them from continuing to seek votes from unpledged delegates or those pledged to candidates who had withdrawn. Thadd, Arnold Pinkney (after Humphrey's withdrawal he worked for me), Charles Evers, Sherry and others kept at it right up to the time of the nominating speeches to increase my total as much as possible: Fauntroy's attempted coup turned out to be a great victory for us. Naturally, many of the black Mc-Govern delegates would still have voted for McGovern, in spite of the caucus action. But others, we were sure, would have gone to me.

To my original 28 delegates, at least 40 previously uncommitted ones had been added before the caucus action, and that total was then enlarged by about 90 former Humphrey delegates. Thadd and the rest of the staff believed they had forty or fifty more votes on the first ballot and were expecting perhaps a hundred more if a second ballot were necessary.

In the actual roll call, the high point my total reached was

151.25 votes. At that point, McGovern passed the 1,415 votes needed for a majority. There were still more states to go, and more votes would have been cast for me, but when McGovern had it clinched, the remaining states switched to him, and the convention made the choice unanimous.

No other woman candidate had ever been given so many votes at a major party convention. Much of the new support had come from Southern delegates; a plurality of the Louisiana delegation switched to me, and more votes came from South Carolina, Tennessee, Mississippi and Georgia. Their intention was to give a demonstration of black unity and potential strength, even if it was too late and too small for the demonstration to be effective. But Northern black delegates and most national black leaders did not go along with the plan. Black delegates from Pennsylvania, Illinois and Massachusetts jumped on the McGovern bandwagon. I could not help feeling that Northern blacks do not appreciate the importance of political unity the way Southerners do; in the South the struggle for economic survival is more intense and leaves less time for playing political games. Having been denied the ballot for so long, Southerners appreciate its value and are less ready to squander it on some candidate who has made vague, verbal commitments but has given no clear, binding promises to prove that he has their interests at heart. As Charles Evers said in seconding my nomination, "I would like to beg you [black delegates] to vote for Shirley Chisholm on the first ballot so the black poor and other people who have been left out for so long will not be in someone's pocket on the first ballot."

This gesture was all that remained of the idea of a black coalition. It had no effect on the convention's outcome. Since that week in July I have sometimes wondered what would have happened if the black bloc had formed and agreed on a strategy; would the outcome have been different? What would the black caucus have accomplished? The choice of the convention would probably not have changed at that late date. McGovern would almost certainly have been nominated and gone on to lose, as he did. But there would have been a beginning made; the black minority would have shown that it could rise above its divisions and act as a force to be reckoned with, and would have been four years closer to the goal of unity. Now it will all have to be done over again in 1975 and 1976; a historic opportunity was lost.

The question of what I would have had the black caucus do should be answered. First, I want to make the point for the record that I never laid down a detailed program because I did not believe it would have been right to try to call the shots. I believe the black caucus should have done *whatever it decided to do,* and my role would have been no greater than anyone else's in deciding what that should have been. My function would have been that of a rallying point, a catalyst, not that of a strong leader. I had, through much of the campaign, a clear idea in my mind of what the caucus should do, and in many respects it was identical to the programs of others; we should ask and get specific pledges of support for programs, like welfare reform, job training, equalization of educational opportunity, an aggressive federal policy on job discrimination, a multiplication of efforts to provide decent housing, and we should get specific pledges of appointments of minority-group members to key executive positions involved with these needs of minorities.

But in one respect I had a different goal, and I want to explain what that was. I did not think any of the potential nominees could be a winner against the astute, entrenched Republican President; Nixon and his well-financed, highly sophisticated campaigners would make maximum effective use of the power of his office to manipulate events and grab the front pages. We didn't have a candidate who could stand up to that. The basic truth that I think I perceived more clearly than some other black politicians in 1971 and 1972, and more than many women's leaders, Hispano-Americans and so on, was that all our efforts would amount to no more than children's games if Richard Nixon were reelected. A winning ticket had to be our overriding concern, even at the temporary cost of other specific goals. There was only one potential winning combination, as I analyzed the election, and I still believe I was right about it: Senator Edward M. Kennedy and Representative Wilbur D. Mills of Arkansas.

Kennedy seems to have been sincere in his repeated statements that he would not run and would not accept the nomination. But if the convention had turned to him, it is hard to believe that he would have rejected the offer. He is a man who could have captured the attention and the votes of the American people in the face of such a campaign as the one Nixon waged; he was our only hope of having a winner, and he would have been far more sympathetic and effective in dealing with the needs of minorities than Nixon, and that was what counted. He was the best choice because he was the only potential winner.

But Kennedy would not have been a winner without Wilbur Mills on the ticket, or someone much like Mills, if there is any such person. Kennedy would not have run as strongly in the North as John F. Kennedy would have, in a second campaign, or as Robert F. Kennedy would have, if he had lived. His automobile accident in 1969 and his never-fully-explained behavior after it will haunt him for the rest of his political life, and beyond that, he has never been as popular a figure as his older brothers. But he would have pulled back Democratic votes that swung to Nixon and gave him the election, something that Muskie and Humphrey would not have been as effective in doing, to my mind. It would not have been enough to win, as long as the South stayed behind Nixon. Here is where Mills comes in. He is the kind of border-state, middle-of-the-road figure who could be acceptable to Southerners and Northerners alike. A more liberal Southerner would have done nothing to balance the ticket. Some like Reubin Askew, Terry Sanford or Jimmy Carter would go down better in the North, but other Southern political leaders and many voters would not have bought them. No more than any other Kennedy would the Senator have had a chance of carrying the South on his own, but Mills would have had a fighting chance of holding it, or at least of keeping it from falling into the Republicans' laps. And Northern voters (although he would have limited appeal for them) would have no reason to vote against him. I could think of no one else who was of national stature, acceptable to North and South alike, who would have filled the bill.

This analysis agreed exactly with Mills' own assessment of the upcoming election. It was for that reason that he had launched a Mills for President campaign, to be in a position to exert some influence in swinging the convention to Kennedy should it deadlock. He was probably surprised and perhaps even amused to learn that I had arrived at the same position independently and was going around touting a Kennedy-Mills ticket. He knew that my position was making me even more unpopular; people were behaving as though I had turned reactionary, or was out to destroy McGovern; and he knew that I was doing it entirely on my own, for no other reason than that I believed the combination to be the key to winning the White House. For me to be advocating Mills certainly would have made him more acceptable to a lot of Northern delegates, and this he knew well too.

The attacks from other black leaders were sometimes sharp. "What's she doing supporting that cracker?" I am told one Congressional Black Caucus member said. They did not like the chance that Texas, Alabama, Louisiana and the rest of the South were moving toward Nixon, but they did not

follow my reasoning on the way to stop it. Mills did understand, and it is likely that Kennedy did; I cannot say, because I
never had any communication with him about it, at any time.
Some of his people told some of mine that the Senator appreciated my sentiments but he was really not interested in running, and that was the limit of our contact. I have never had
close ties with the Kennedy family; quite the reverse, because
I was never prepared to be one of their blacks. My support
was purely pragmatic politics. Mills appreciated this even
more because he knew that I was knowingly risking attacks
from other blacks by my stand; he considered that it was a
brave thing I was doing, solely for the sake of party victory,
and probably his opinion of my political sense improved a
great deal as a result. Mills and I agreed that if blacks, not to
mention the rest of the country, wanted another four years of
Nixon, the way to get them was to nominate a loser and fight
to keep a Southerner off the ticket.

After McGovern's nomination, there was a brief boomlet
for putting a woman or a black on the ticket as Vice President. Naturally, I was mentioned, but I squelched the idea.
McGovern, I said, has a right to pick his own Vice President.
The most intense maneuvering was inside the women's caucus and centered on Frances "Sissy" Farenthold of Texas. It
was a gesture much like the one some blacks had made in
voting for me. The whole convention had been a bitter disappointment to many delegates from the women's movement
point of view; it had been organized from the start by the

McGovern people to make sure that no group could upset the plan to nominate the South Dakota Senator. As much as blacks, women and their interests had suffered. McGovern's people double-crossed women on a challenge to the South Carolina delegation; women were under-represented in it, and the women's caucus regarded the challenge as the key test of their campaign for fair representation. McGovern had told the National Women's Political Caucus that he unequivocally supported their challenge. The NWPC wanted to eliminate nine men from the South Carolina contingent and replace them with nine women. The vote promised to be close; other Southern states and some Northern ones wanted the challenge to fail because their own delegations would be exposed to change if it succeeded. The women would have a slim majority if McGovern's delegates backed them. But McGovern strategists did not dare. There was a serious parliamentary question whether a majority on the crucial California challenge meant a majority of the whole number of delegates at the convention, or a majority of those from the other states and territories with California not voting on its own case. The chair had not ruled and McGovern did not want it to rule, because he feared the decision would be that an absolute majority was required, and on that basis he could lose. If the South Carolina challenge vote was close, someone, perhaps a Southerner, would demand a ruling. So McGovern had to see that the vote was not close enough for that to happen. Gary Hart, his national campaign manager, manipulated

McGovern votes throughout a long roll call on the question. The strategy worked. McGovern's position was secure for the California vote, but the pledge to women had been thrown overboard to save the ship.

A second disappointment for the women's forces was over an abortion plank they wanted in the platform. In this case, it was not at first a matter of McGovern's reneging on a promise, because he had not made one. In fact, he had tried all along to keep the abortion question out of his campaign. He did not believe that it was a matter for each woman and her conscience to decide; the argument that women have a right to control their own bodies never seemed to impress McGovern. Many women, including Gloria Steinem, Bella Abzug and Betty Friedan, had tried to convert him, but McGovern slipped away without making a commitment. The Platform Committee at its meeting in Washington had had a long, involved debate that ended in no action. Having lost South Carolina, Steinem and others were determined to make a fight to write an abortion plank into the Democratic platform.

At first the McGovern strategists said they would keep hands off the issue and let it be "a vote of conscience" for each delegate. But this was not to be; as the story is told by an insider, actress Shirley MacLaine (who had deserted her own principles as a member of the women's movement to help the McGovern men maneuver and keep the issue out of the campaign), the trouble started when someone learned that the North Carolina delegation was going to vote yes on a strong abortion plank. One must remember that it was late in the night; early in the morning, actually, going on 5:00 A.M. after an all-night session that started late on Tuesday evening. MacLaine recalls hearing Pierre Salinger tell California leader Willie Brown, "The fix is in." Fatigue, tension, and poor communications were breeding paranoia, and the McGovernites thought they saw a new conspiracy against them by Hubert H. Humphrey, George C. Wallace and others: they were out to get revenge by hanging an abortion plank around McGovern's neck like an albatross. It was a foolish thought; Humphrey would never have been part of such a scheme, nor would Henry M. Jackson nor I, and I do not believe George Wallace would, although he might have been amused by the idea and let some of his supporters go ahead with it if they wanted to. The truth was later discovered: a North Carolina woman named Martha McKay had simply been lobbying the men in her delegation and had swung a number of them to support the abortion plank.

But Brown, Salinger, Gary Hart and the rest of McGovern's floor strategists did not know that, so they began cracking the whip over their delegates: "Vote against the minority plank on abortion. It will kill George if they get that in." Arms were twisted all over the floor. The plank, which probably would have been defeated even if McGovern had honored his promise to keep aloof, was heavily defeated. Abzug, Steinem and others were furious. They had considered McGovern wishy-washy on abortion, but now they felt betrayed. Like the blacks, the women had failed to get it together at Miami; too many had made commitments to a candidate ahead of time, and their adherence to him made it impossible for them to work effectively for their cause. Women like Shirley MacLaine and blacks like Willie Brown were the targets of accusations that they had sold out to McGovern. It seems to me that "sold out" is the wrong interpretation; they were not bought. They gave themselves away.

Through all of this, I was not on the floor; I spent most of the time seeing people in my hotel rooms. I went to Convention Hall only to make my acceptance speech Wednesday night and on Thursday night to appear with the other unsuccessful candidates on the platform as a display of unity behind the nominee. "The only thing to do now is to work as hard as we can to elect George McGovern," I told my staff and any former supporters who came to see me. To those who commiserated with me on the way the campaign turned out, I said, "Let's just say this has been a wonderful trip we have taken together. There have been lots of mistakes. If we did it again, we would do it differently right from the start."

XI

McGovern and the Campaign

JULY WENT BY, and August, and I waited to hear from McGovern. My initial eagerness to campaign for him against Nixon began to die down. A black national campaign steering committee was formed, but no one invited me to help. It became clear what the attitude of the McGovern organization was toward me. I had been against them on California, so I was an enemy; there was nothing I could do for them; they wanted no part of me. This attitude extended to people on my staff and former supporters who offered to work for McGovern, some of them repeatedly, and were rebuffed. "What's the matter with the people around McGovern?" one asked me. "Don't they know he's in trouble and they need all the help they can get?"

At first I found it hard to believe the stories I heard about McGovern's organization turning away help, but when it happened to some of my own supporters and staff people, I could no longer doubt. The McGovern campaign was dominated by arrogant white intellectuals. After Miami they became overconfident; they had come so far against the odds that they knew they could go the rest of the way against the odds. They disdained alliances with anyone who could not meet their standards of purity and loyalty; they could not trust anyone who had not been, in the phrase we kept hearing, "with George right from the start." There was something religious about it; one felt they saw themselves as an island of light in a sea of darkness, or champions of truth and goodness surrounded by evil conspirators. As the campaign progressed McGovern seemed to absorb the attitude and transmitted it in his speeches.

Winning a general election can be quite different from winning a primary, except when one party is in a dominant position. A primary can be won by mobilizing a minority, as McGovern did. But to win a general election takes a broader appeal, and this McGovern could never seem to muster. He did not win over the minorities, and his efforts to do so were the most ill-conceived parts of his campaign. He doled out money to self-appointed "black leaders" for registration drives, and a number of them were hustlers who took it and ran. If tax money had been involved, it would have been a major scandal that they did not put on the registration drives they were paid to conduct. In the South, on the other hand, there were to be no funds for registration; McGovern wrote off the South completely. In Mississippi I know the machinery was there to push registration; Dr. Aaron Henry, the state chairman, pleaded for funds to put it to work and got scant attention from McGovern's Southern regional coordinator.

McGovern had no strategy for reaching the minorities. His

black steering committee never came up with one. Another problem was that the candidate never seemed at ease with black people. Perhaps it was reserve and shyness, but there seemed to be a hesitancy about his social contacts with blacks that they could not help but sense. It could be because they are few and far between in the West, where he grew up, and he had never had many black friends. It was a marked difference in him and Humphrey, Lindsay or Muskie.

Like the minority groups, labor, women, older voters and noncollege young people were not won over to McGovern, and the reason was similar: he and the young, white, middle-class leaders of his staff were way out of touch with what these voters wanted. They thought they knew it all, much like the young anti-poverty workers who went out from the Office of Equal Opportunity in the 1960s with the answers to poverty and community problems. Except for Anne Wexler, women in McGovern's organization were all in subordinate jobs, and at that they were like the men: white, college-trained, middle-class. Where were the welfare mothers to articulate their needs? Where were the Indians and Chicanos? What did McGovern's young people know about the two-thirds of their age group who did not finish college but were working and starting families? There were a number of labor leaders for McGovern, in spite of George Meany's withholding the AFL-CIO's backing, but they too seem to have been out of touch with the mass of organized workers. Meany may have reflected the views of labor as a whole much better than McGovern and the liberal columnists believed at the time. The McGovernites believed they were forming a coalition, but they did not; they did not have a coalition going into Miami and they never developed one afterward. The McGovern campaign remained a minority movement. This was fatal, because it was not a Democratic Party campaign; the McGovernites had offended and eliminated many of the local leaders they would have needed for a party-line effort. Mayor Richard J. Daley of Chicago is the best known and biggest example, but there were many others in smaller cities and counties. To some extent they had to do it, because the leaders tended to back Humphrey, Muskie or Jackson, and both sides cannot win an election. But after the primaries and especially after the convention, there was too little effort to heal the breach and get the local leaders' allegiance. The McGovernites' alienation of the pros was to a large extent deliberate, as well; it was a reaction to the 1968 Democratic convention, where many of McGovern's key staffers were McCarthy or Kennedy boosters and had seen or even suffered what happened there—the beating and gassing in the streets, the steamroller for Humphrey on the floor. They came away with the lesson that the pros were not to be trusted; so nearly anyone with political experience was excluded from the "new Democratic Party."

What makes the outcome of the campaign tragic, in my view, is that I shared McGovern's views on the preponderance of the issues. Of all the candidates, he and I were in the closest agreement on the war. We had both been for years in the Congressional minority that was determined to end it by any means and turn the money it was wasting into social programs. We agreed on cutting the defense budget, on welfare reform and on the need to create jobs and train people for them. I was disappointed at his equivocation on school busing for the purpose of desegregation, and I felt that his views on the Middle East were a little naïve. But these points of difference were not enough to outweigh the overall sympathy I had for his position.

McGovern was the man I would most have liked to see in the White House, out of the field of candidates available to the party in 1972. But he was not the man I judged the best fitted to get there. He did not look to me like a winner in March, and he did not look like one in July. By October, there was no doubt about it. He was headed for a crushing defeat that he had, in some ways, richly deserved, and this would be a great loss for the country. I wish McGovern had made a more determined effort, starting in July, to involve in his campaign all the elements of the party that he had alienated or rejected. I was not among the alienated; I had no reservations whatever about working for George, and I would have done whatever he asked. But he did not ask until late in the campaign, and then it was only to appear with him on a trip to Philadelphia, continuing on to Brooklyn. There was a strong suspicion in my mind that the reason was that his chief black lieutenants were many of the same men who had promoted the various black coalition meetings during 1971 and 1972—Walter Fauntroy, Julian Bond, Jesse Jackson, Representative Louis Stokes and others.

If my name was mentioned in strategy meetings, I believe they gave him adverse reactions. "It would be better if you didn't have to deal with her," they probably said, and McGovern may have felt he would lose them if he worked with me.

The important thing is that the views McGovern and I advocated during the campaign must not be discredited by his crushing defeat. Richard Nixon won in forty-nine states by, for one thing, appealing to the inherent racism of the American people. Voters saw him—a Harris poll two months after the election showed this plainly—as the candidate who would put a stop to school busing and the encroachment of blacks and other minorities on white jobs and neighborhoods. McGovern may have double-talked on the busing issue, but there was no real doubt that he and Nixon stood for opposite views. It will be catastrophic for this country, which has sometimes seemed to be poised on the brink of racial and class war, if the Nixon approach becomes the stock campaign strategy of both parties. Candidates then would do what Democrats did in the South for years—campaign by competing to see who could yell "Nigger!" the loudest. In Michigan Congressional contests in 1972, this phenomenon was already occurring, and among those who betrayed everything they had stood for were such one-time civil rights advocates as Representative James O'Hara and Representative William D. Ford.

Men like George McGovern and Hubert H. Humphrey are going to be badly needed in the U.S. Senate in the coming years. Our public life would be greatly enhanced if we had dozens more George McGoverns, men who, to quote George Orwell, are "generously angry—a free intelligence, a type hated with equal hatred by all the little orthodoxies which are now contending for our souls."

The pity of the campaign was that McGovern did not *seem* to be the man he really was. His image was distorted beyond repair in the California campaign by a fellow liberal who must bear part of the blame for what happened later. In California, Hubert H. Humphrey sounded the themes that Republicans were to seize on and elaborate. He found McGovern's weak spots and exploited them, showing the opposition how to destroy him when he became the candidate. Humphrey hung the millstone of McGovern's first, poorly thought-out welfare proposals (the famous "$1,000 for everyone" plan) forever around the South Dakota Senator's neck, and he helped create the impression that McGovern was the candidate of "acid, abortion and amnesty." Humphrey himself did not engage in such a low, direct attack as that "three-A" characterization, but he came close enough to it to show the Nixon camp how effective it could be.

The Thomas Eagleton affair was not in itself sufficient to account for McGovern's defeat. McGovern's Hamlet-like behavior after the Missouri Senator's one-time mental health problems became public certainly helped increase a popular conception that he was irresolute in a crisis. The McGovern staff, it has since been learned, knew about it before McGovern did, but did not inform him, which could be another effect of their inexperience. Once the initial decision was made to select Eagleton, there was no longer any way for him to get out with a whole skin, and this was the reason for his apparent wavering. One cannot help but wonder why Eagleton did not inform McGovern, before allowing his name to be placed in nomination, that he had once received shock treatments for depression. If any blame attaches to anyone in the whole affair, it probably should be to Eagleton, and yet he seems to have emerged as the only hero.

Could it be that the qualities that make a good campaigner are not necessarily those that make a good President? McGovern, as I have said, would have been the best choice by far. But Americans seem to demand affable, outgoing politicians who can sing with the Irish, kibitz with the Jews, preach in a black church and dance at a Polish wedding, then charm the ladies at a suburban shopping center. Unhappily for George McGovern, the Democratic Party and most of all the country, this kind of thing was not his forte. As one woman lamented, "He comes across like cream cheese."

The result was a forty-nine-state landslide for Richard M. Nixon, which the President clearly took as a mandate to rule the country as he saw fit. By the end of 1972 he had outraged many of his former supporters by ordering devastating new bombing raids on North Vietnam, killing hundreds and thousands of civilians and increasing the cost of the war by close to a billion dollars—the war that, just before the election, had seemed to be over at last. It seemed undeniable that the forecasts of peace had been a political maneuver. His victory secured at home with the tactic, he proceeded to chase the fox-fire of victory in Vietnam with the same methods that had been failing for six years and more, attempting with military might to compel the North Vietnamese to accept peace on our terms.

All this was horrible enough, but Nixon's moves in domestic policy were even more threatening. He reshuffled his Cabinet to put people in key positions who would be loyal and subservient, pliable secretaries who would not question his decisions and rock the ship of state, even to the limited extent that a few members of the administration did in the first term. He embarked on a policy of drastic reduction of social programs in the name of economy—housing, employment and education spending cut across the board, programs wiped out or crippled for lack of funds. Richard M. Nixon was out to make his place in history; having opened relations with the People's Republic of China and improved those with the Soviet Union, he intended to set to rights what he regarded as a runaway federal budget and a grossly ineffective, hypertrophied and wasteful government establishment. His approach to the problem was, predictably, to lop off social programs first and everywhere. Whether Congress could block him, if it would, was doubtful. My conclusion about it all was that he has a deeper concern for his place in history than for the people he governs. And history will not fail to note that fact.

XII.

Black Alternatives

MANY OF THE 1972 McGovern backers and many of the Chisholm Trail-hands of that year have now reached the conclusion that, having tried to influence national politics and failed, their course should be to plunge into local politics and try to influence city and county elections, to organize tenants and farmworkers, and to build up minority political organizations. I think this is a sound instinct and a worthwhile effort. Presidential politics is a big-time, high-stakes game, and it is played by tough, sophisticated politicians with plenty of money and plenty of skill. My own participation in it in 1971 and 1972 was a unique, one-shot phenomenon, an effort by an amateur supported by a crowd of idealists. We were out to make a mark, but we could not hope to win; we didn't have what it takes, and we knew it from the start. I would not recommend that any woman, or any black or Hispano-American, ever do again exactly what I did. The next campaign by a woman or a black must be well prepared and well financed; it must be planned long in advance, and it must aim at the building of a new national coalition. This is a subject I will return to, but for a moment I would like to discuss what I see as the most promising direction for blacks and other minority political groups in the coming years. To do so, we should consider first where we have been and where we are now.

Modern black politics began on a specific date, February 1, 1960, when four freshmen at the all-black North Carolina Agricultural and Technical College in Greensboro sat down at a lunch counter in a Woolworth store and ordered four cups of coffee. They were protesting the fact that they could buy paper and toothpaste at the store but could not be served at its lunch counter. The world "protesting" sounds familiar today, but in 1960 it was a strange, new term. Mahatma Gandhi had used the sit-in technique during his years of struggle against the British rule of India, and the Congress of Racial Equality had taken the idea from him and used it in Chicago. But it did not attract much public attention until the 1960 sit-ins in Greensboro. The essential elements of the technique were two: it was a moral protest, and it involved direct action. The moral issue at stake was racism of the most hypocritical kind; the store was not above profiting from the black students' needs, but it would not serve them at its lunch counter. Second, it was action, not talk—simple, direct action that illustrated what it was meant to prove. Both themes had appeared in the Montgomery bus boycott, when Mrs. Rosa Parks sat down at the front of a bus, and thousands of black citizens supported her by declaring, through their actions, "If you will not treat us like human beings, we will not ride in your buses." The technique outraged white liberals at first. The famous Ralph McGill, editor of the Atlanta *Constitution,* denounced it. Later on he had to admit that it was "productive of the most change" of any tactic that had been tried. "No argument in a court of law could have dramatized the immorality and irrationality of a custom as did the sit-in," he wrote in his book, *The South and the Southerner,* ". . . not even the Supreme Court decision on schools in 1954."

There followed a brief few years in which whites and blacks, most of them college students, enthusiastically cooperated in direct-action attacks on racist institutions and individuals. There were Freedom Rides and Freedom Walks, and voter registration drives through the South. It was an amazing and apparently spontaneous transformation in the attitudes and behavior of youth; the generation of the 1950s had been so famous for its "apathy" that some college newspapers banned the overused word from their editorials. Now it was enlisting en masse in a high-minded and high-spirited campaign to integrate the society by living and fighting together, going to jail together, and sometimes (this must never be forgotten) dying together.

But the civil rights movement did not achieve its lofty ideals. Hotels and buses were desegregated, but blacks perceived slowly that they were not much better off than before. What good is it to be allowed to sit in the front of the

bus when you haven't got the fare? Inevitably, the movement fell apart along racial lines. The blacks began to see
that they were still, subtly, being treated as inferiors by the
white students. They were in the same position that Frederick Douglass found himself in a century earlier with the
famous abolitionist William Lloyd Garrison. The well-
meaning Garrison was using Douglass as an "exhibition
piece," Douglass perceived, and when the great black leader
demanded a more important role in the abolition movement, Garrison said he thought that the most black people
were able to do at the moment was to serve as exhibits of
the fact that they could be taught to read, write and speak
about their experiences as slaves. Douglass understood then
that he was still in a master-slave relationship with the white
man and resolved to break his intellectual chains as well as
his physical ones. Young blacks in the 1960s played out the
same story. Where they had been integrationist and nonvi-
olent, they became separatist and militant. It was the era of
Black Power. Discovering that they were not going to win
any important gains by carrying picket signs and coaching
people for literacy tests, they declared their independence
from white society in every way. In diet, dress, religion,
clothing and behavior, they set out to become black, black
and beautiful, black and proud.

This struck a deep chord in the soul of black Americans, whose great need is to believe in their worth and dignity, their selfhood, after generations of having been beaten,
sold, murdered, exploited and demeaned. They have been

told in the most direct, brutal ways that they are worthless, and there are deep psychic wounds in the minds of all black Americans. A few hard-won gains in status have not healed them, and healing them is the most important priority for blacks. Independence movements, from community-united black fronts to the Black Panthers and the Republic of New Africa—each has an essential role to play in the cure. Of course, one may criticize some of their tactics. I have, myself; but it should not be missed that the people who hate and fear the militant black movements the most, and who would mobilize all the resources of the law against them, do not come with clean hands; they are people who have profited through the years from black subjugation. Many of them have supported in the past, by inaction or action, a group that was far worse than the most militant black ones, the Ku Klux Klan.

Before long, a more sophisticated and forward-looking concept of black power began to develop. Christopher Lasch in his book, *The Agony of the American Left,* summarizes it neatly: "What black power proposes is that blacks do for themselves what other ethnic groups faced with similar conditions have done." The naïve conception once taught, and perhaps taught still in the public schools, was that America is a "melting pot." It has become clear in the last two decades that this was never true, that American society is instead a "mosaic" of elements that exist side by side but have never lost their identities. The minorities—Germans, Jews, Irish, Italians, Greeks, Slavs—have not been assimilated into the population after two or three generations. Every big city politician knows this; ethnic voting blocs are a fact of life for him, and a great deal of attention is paid to ticket-balancing as a way of dealing with them. Something is provided for the Irish Catholic vote, something for the Jewish vote, and so on.

Black Americans have obviously been a more stubbornly unassimilable group than any of the others. But the point is that this is not the problem. Eventually all the groups may be assimilated, in two hundred or a thousand years. I do not think they will, but that does not matter. The point is that it is not going to happen soon, and that assimilation should not be the goal even if it were possible. How did the other groups escape from their ghettos? That is the question. It was by building up their economic and political power, and they did that by keeping and building on their identity as a separate group.

Look at the Irish in Boston, who came there, to quote a biographer of John F. Kennedy, "as the lowest of the low, lower than the Germans or the Scandinavians or the Jews, or even Negroes who had come early and edged a bit up the economic ladder." Lasch in his book makes the point that the Irish were not liberated by individually overcoming the barriers put up by white New England society. They began by operating on the margins, working at jobs like ditch-digging that they were allowed to take, operating small businesses—little banks with an ethnic clientele, small stores, taverns. They built a society inside the larger society.

When they advanced, they did not do so as individuals, although certain individuals led the way. They advanced as a group, and as they did they helped perfect an institution that has become basic in American life: ward or "machine" politics. Their political organizations became factors that the established community leaders had to deal with and make concessions to, and in most places they still do. In less than four generations, the despised Boston Irish produced mayors, Senators and at last a President. And they did it by being more aggressively and indelibly Irish, not by turning themselves into Brahmins.

Here we have the first principle of political action for blacks, Chicanos, Indians and other minorities: be yourselves. In the perspective of long-range goals of social order and progress, it may seem like a step backward. But it is a necessary step politically, economically, culturally and psychologically. It is particularly so politically. Politics is the only route to power, and even in the most democratic society, power is the name of the game. Power makes, interprets and enforces the laws. It decides what interests shall flourish and which shall perish. It determines who will be educated and how much, who may work at what kinds of jobs, where they may live, and what they may do and with whom. So the slogans must be "Black Power!" and "I am somebody," "Red Power" and *La Raza Unida* and *Huelga!* Separation and self-assertion is not the ultimate goal; it is a strategy. It is at once the recognition of a fact—separation has always existed in this society—and the expression of a deep need, to be regarded as a unique, valuable and individual human being. Separation in the past has always served white majority interests. It has created *barrios* and black slums to be pools of cheap domestic and hand labor, and used the myth of white superiority to maintain them. Whites think quite often that Black Power and *La Raza Unida* and other phrases are assertions of black superiority and calls for revolutions. Let us pause a moment to dispose of this myth of revolution. It is neither practical nor desirable. First, a revolution by any minority is a mad idea because it cannot succeed. The power of the modern corporate state, backed by its police, armies and National Guards, is too overwhelming; it would surround any rebellion with a steel ring of tanks and bayonets and crush it out. But second, it is a wrong philosophy because, for the revolutionaries, it would mean becoming as corrupt and inhuman as the elements they seek to overturn. Killing, hatred, conspiracy and violence are what we must eliminate, not foster.

What can be done is to take the situation imposed by the majority, the separateness into which we have been forced, and turn it into a political, economic and cultural weapon. The task of the black community is to redefine itself and create its own values and goals, then organize to win them. This is the path that many blacks, instinctively or by conscious design, are now taking. They are beginning to come together, find leaders and act to reduce black dependency and put themselves in a position to bargain rather than to beg—not to dictate, but to bargain.

There are pitfalls along the way. It is easy to mistake talk for action. Too many people are going around with naturals and dashikis talking black and doing nothing. They are jiving the people in a new way that is just as bad as the old jive white liberals passed out for years. Their goal is to glorify themselves. I do not need to name them; there are too many to select a few for reprobation, because a large percentage of black leaders are this sort. But their day is passing. They are a transient phenomenon. Everywhere, responsible and realistic black people are being discovered by their oppressed brothers and sisters and put forward into positions of real importance, in city councils and school boards, in mayors' offices and state legislatures. The number of black elected officials grows with every election. Protests and separatist movements had their day and played their part, but now black Americans—and all the other minorities—have begun to shift their primary goal to full political participation. They will succeed, of course, only as far as they can achieve unity. They have to come together at specific times for specific reasons.

I am not extolling unity on everything and in every situation; this is a fantasy that has never happened and never will. Face facts: any time you try to get black people on any single block together, you discover how difficult it is to get them to commit themselves to any one thing. Blacks have to learn to make individual commitments to the common needs and relinquish some of their individual needs and goals temporarily to the common cause, to achieve effective political action. There is nothing wrong with Afros and dashikis, or with processed hair and white shirts and ties. What is wrong are actions that separate black people instead of bringing them together. If we are out to recapture our African heritage, that can be a fine thing, but let us not think it consists in studying Swahili or putting tribal sculpture on the wall. Instead let us understand and re-create the African's extended family ties, his closeness to the earth, his sense of group responsibility, his respect for the aged and his reverence for life. These things are the true soul of black people, and they can be expressed as well in the conservative, go-to-work six days, church-going black family's life as they can in the most "African" style of living. It is in the heart of the black individual and in the home of each black family that the process of becoming truly black and proud must take place. Strong family units will make strong and secure neighborhoods; they will result in a strong black society capable of combating the social pressures and challenges of this time and place.

Putting black power into political action will demand preparation. Of course the white majority has been insensitive and repressive, socially, economically and politically; of course it has not responded enough to the minorities' needs. But until now black people have not responded enough either, or done enough in the area of practical politics. I do not mean the old-style "you help me, I'll do something for you" politics; I mean the kind that builds mass awareness of what is needed and what can really be done about it, that finds natural, effective leaders and supports them. I mean real, participatory, democratic political action. Organize, plan, register, campaign and vote. The machinery for effective action is all in place. We have only to put our hands on it and use it.

The obstacles to effective, unified black action are about the same as those people of every race encounter when they try to join in a cooperative effort: lack of vision, unexamined prejudices and concentration on personal desires at the expense of the common goal. Working together means getting out of the nine-to-five, draw-your-pay, drink-some-beer-and-watch-television routine. It means becoming more aware of the world and society we live in and the people in it, developing deeper, more meaningful interrelations and, through them, coming to understand the purpose of our own existence. All these things are involved in the meaning of black power; but they are the same things involved in achieving full humanity and responsible citizenship for people of any color. In the end, the establishment of black pride and power will liberate whites as well as blacks; both have been less than fully human in their dealings with each other. Just as men will be freed when women are liberated, blacks and whites will emerge as more vital and ennobled beings when they can meet each other face to face as men and women of equal worth and potential.

XIII.

Coalition Politics

THERE IS A good deal of evidence that the United States is moving to the right, and that the main force behind the movement is a resurgence, in a new form, of racial prejudice. The desegregation of buses, restaurants and public drinking fountains was succeeded by efforts to desegregate schools, jobs and neighborhoods, and a strong backlash reaction was the result. I cannot view President Nixon's landslide reelection as anything but an effect of this dangerous and profoundly anti-democratic strain in the American character. The election of mayors in Philadelphia, Minneapolis and Los Angeles who had set their campaign sails to the same wind shows that there is a strong force involved, and we must expect that it will continue to be felt in city, state, Congressional and Presidential elections. Older Americans are afraid of what is happening. They are not ready to accept blacks and other minorities into their unions, clubs and neighborhoods. They hide their motives from themselves by using code phrases like "forced busing," "law and order" and "welfare chiselers." But there is real fear in many white breasts, and it is going to make the going hard for the movement toward justice and equal opportunity for both sexes and all races. One can realistically foresee increasing repression and neglect of social evils like poverty and unequal job opportunities, and this will call forth in turn increasing alienation and rebellion among black, Puerto Rican and other groups that remain excluded from full participation in the economic, social and political life of the country. I have just sketched the first steps I think minority groups should take to deal with the problem politically; now let us go further and explore how, in the face of the growing divisions that afflict our country, it may be possible for groups with differences to work together.

The old political parties were once a device that made cooperation between divergent elements to some extent possible. They usually worked on a quid pro quo basis: you vote for me, and I'll help your brother get a job in the Parks Department—that kind of thing. There was a great deal to be said for machine politics at one period in our evolution. It was, at least, a way for the poor and powerless to bargain for some limited gains in their lot; they knew who was in control and they knew how the bosses could be dealt with, by trading allegiance for favors. Patronage and loyalty: they were the twin pillars of the system. It is vanishing now; many people have helped to kill it, among them myself and others in Brooklyn in the last two decades. But what will take its place?

One has to look at things in the perspective of one's own experience. I come out of the New York City of the 1940s, 1950s and 1960s, when the breakdown of the old clubhouse structure was replaced by something variously called fusion or coalition politics. Fiorello La Guardia probably started it; the Reform Democrats of the 1940s carried on the tradition, and John V. Lindsay, in his second campaign, succeeded in reviving the concept enough to win reelection against the forces of both regular parties. He could never repeat the triumph now, but this is not entirely his fault. It tells us something about coalition politics, that alignments are forever shifting, that today's enemies can be tomorrow's allies, and of course the reverse.

The translation of local coalition politics into the formation of a national coalition is not an easy thing to envision. The two major parties have continued to control national politics—Presidential and to a large degree Congressional campaigns—because nothing has emerged to take their place. It is hardly necessary to point out that they have been working less and less well; either one is barely recognizable compared with itself twenty years ago. The South is going Republican—one can almost say "has gone." Many formerly staunch Democratic voting blocs are now swing votes—labor, Jews, Catholics. There seems to be more and more a tendency for the Midwest to go Democratic on national issues, although it thinks of itself as Republican.

Everything is in ferment and flux. It is possible that the confusion will settle down into new alignments, but one can hardly foretell what they will be. So the question arises, can a new national coalition be created, and if so, what part will blacks, labor and other elements play in it?

The Democratic Party once had a genius for containing diversity and this was the source of its attraction and effectiveness. It has now been torn apart in two successive elections. I see a dialectical process at work. The Chicago convention of 1968 was the thesis, when the old guard crushed the new elements in the party. In 1972, the newcomers crushed the old-timers; they hooted in delight as they drove Mayor Daley and his regular Illinois delegation from the Convention Hall—antithesis, exactly. In each case, one wing of the party viciously throttled the other and excluded it from participation in the campaign. Both ended in defeat. Has that experience taught both the suicidal effect of such behavior, and can a synthesis emerge by 1976?

One can hope so, because both wings must be chastened by now and ready to look for a way to rejoin. But wishes are not horses, or even donkeys. How can it be done? How can blue-collar whites be united with blacks, when they are in competition for jobs? How can intellectual, "limousine liberals" combine with working-class ethnic voters who resent their affluence and easy access to power? One can set up such dichotomies almost without end, until the task seems hopeless. Still, we must look for hope because the alternative is to surrender to further splintering and impotence of the party.

And the other party is not immune to the process, either. Its new adherents in the working class will be uneasy with the wealthy and well-to-do WASPs who control it, and George Wallace demonstrated that there is a sizable group of voters for whom the Republicans are entirely too liberal. But this kind of splintering cannot go on without check, because it will eventually destroy our form of government, and there is little reason I can see to believe that what would come in its place would be in any way an improvement. Our system of representative democracy has never worked right. Too many have been excluded, overlooked and oppressed by it. But it is capable of great flexibility and improvement. There is almost no limit to the extent that it could be reformed to become a truly responsive and representative form of government. This has always been my political faith, which has survived innumerable setbacks and disappointments. I love America not for what she is, but for what she can become. But she is in serious trouble, and to fix it we must start to deny ourselves the kind of self-indulgent, childish public behavior that doomed the McGovern campaign and which strangled the 1972 national black coalition in its infancy.

New politics demands a new kind of leader. Here is the key. The new breed must combine that personal magnetism that was dubbed "charisma" when John F. Kennedy was demonstrating it with something even rarer, the ability to involve on all levels the disparate elements and factions of the groups they lead. Such leaders can be found, formed and thrust forward by the processes through which a coalition comes together and finds its common goals. Or the leader may come first, starting a vision and putting together the elements necessary to make it reality. Either way, such men are easy to recognize. Martin Luther King was one. Cesar Chavez is one. Behind them, the bickering and fighting continue, but when they say the time has come to march, the troops fall in line. McGovern, unfortunately, was not such a man, although many of his people tried to believe he was. He lacked the warmth, the dignity and the *loneliness* that distinguish the true leaders like Chavez, King and Robert F. Kennedy.

But one need not wait for a leader to appear, at least at the local and state level. Coalitions to fight for control of city halls or for creation of neighborhood health centers do not need some commanding figure to step forth and call them into being. The needs are there, and to meet them groups will come together. The combinations will be evanescent and will have to be re-formed for each fresh election, but in this can be their strength. They will keep getting new input of ideas and creative individuals from every crisis and reorganization they undergo; or if they do not, it will mean that their time is past and it is a good thing for them to disappear.

Coalition politics is hard work. It is much easier to set the organization up in hierarchies, with the leader, his lieutenants, their sergeants and the rank and file at the bottom. But a democratic political movement is not an army; it exists only *for the sake* of the ordinary people who make up its body, and the most important consideration is to organize it so it responds to their needs and seeks to fulfill them. Let me illustrate this by citing the McGovern organization as an example of what *not* to do. I have observed before that it included some blacks, but they were not in policy-making positions, and that the same was true of women, Hispano-Americans and so on. The blacks that McGovern (and the other white candidates—I do not except them) had with him were not there because they believed in the man and his programs but because they were bought or rented as tokens. There was no real commitment *from* them because there was no real commitment *to* them. It was just an arrangement for mutual political advantage. Nobody was getting any real input from blacks. They were treating them, as always, like children—find out what they want at that moment and promise it to them, so they'll be good. What most white politicians never suspect is that some of the black "leaders" they recruit may not be leaders at all, but hustlers. The mass of black Americans are different in many ways from their self-appointed spokesmen. For instance, they are very conservative.

This black conservatism is something that surprises many whites, if they ever happen to encounter it. For example, the reason a lot of blacks were opposed to my candidacy was that they did not believe *any black* could be President. They have deep-down feelings of inferiority, which they hide in various ways, some by overvaluing their negritude and some by conservative emulation of white values and customs. Another root of black conservatism is a deep religious feeling. The average black has strong ties to a church, which persist even when he drifts away from its influence. Black ministers have a profound effect on the black masses, and they are basically conservative men. Their faith teaches them not to strive for salvation in this world, but to look beyond it. They preach that all will be well on the other side of Jordan, and so help their congregations escape from the hard daily realities of their lives. Blacks who spend a great deal of time in church are hard to rouse to deal with unpleasant social issues; they believe that God will help them, and that things are as He wills them. It is a touching, mystical and transcendent faith that goes deep in the black soul. I do not mean to belittle it when I observe that it is also an attitude perfectly calculated to pacify slaves.

The black church never got involved with political and social problems until Martin Luther King and some of the men of his generation did. Then there were marches and sit-ins, organized in the churches partly because black people had nowhere else to get together and talk. And, of course, the church bombings followed.

To a lot of black people I am a real radical, and they never could support me. Imagine how they feel about all-out black radicals of the kind most prominent in national politics.

I have dwelt at length on this point because it illustrates what I have said earlier and repeat now, that the white would-be leaders of coalitions cannot know very much about blacks if they do not have a feeling for their innate conservatism and piety. Blacks have equally erroneous perceptions of whites, and college students have them of trade unionists, and so on. The only way to correct such misconceptions and get groups working in harmony is to throw them together and let the differences emerge and be worked out. The process will fail oftener than it succeeds, perhaps, but we must keep trying. Equality of status and mutual respect: those are the prerequisites for forming a successful coalition of groups. Submergence of personal goals and demands at times, where necessary to stay together on other projects, will be vital. Some women were able to give up their belief in abortion on demand for the sake of George McGovern's candidacy; one can disagree with their having done this, but not with the principle behind their action. That is the way to make political gains. Some groups that are campaigning for a $6,500-a-year guaranteed annual income to replace the rotten welfare system have never been able to function effectively as a political force because they are completely intransigent in their demands; it is that or nothing. So they get nothing. This is the kind of apocalyptic thinking that people can fall into when they have no political experience whatever, and it is quite pardonable because blacks, poor people, women and others have never had an opportunity to gain sophistication in politics.

Formation of a new national coalition will be far more difficult than the formation of one at the level of a city or a school district. I am not even prepared to say it is possible. But it is essential, and so we must try. I do not have a recipe,

but I can see a few ways to start. There need not be such
enmity between trade unionists and aspiring blacks over
jobs; the problem is not built into the people involved but
exists in the situation that there are not now enough jobs
for everyone. But there are endless needs that would take
the hands of every able person to fill—cities to rebuild, land
to reclaim and preserve, hospitals and houses to provide for
a growing population. The synthesis of these two warring
elements is in getting them to see that they have a common
need—decent, satisfying, respectable, paying jobs to do.
Then they can join—setting their other differences aside
temporarily—to do something about correcting an arrangement in which idle people and great needs for their labor
exist side by side. Not every pair of opposing groups can
be reconciled this way, but many of them can; there is not
really as much difference between them as it now appears.
All human beings share a great many more similarities than
they have differences.

Will the Democratic Party be the vehicle for forming
a new coalition? Not necessarily, but there is more to be
said for trying to rebuild and reform it than for replacing
it. First, it is there—on the ballot in every state and county,
which is no small matter, as any candidate for a minority
party can testify. Second, it contains many of the potential
elements of a new combination of forces and should be acceptable to almost any of the others. One major contradic-
tion within the party has been easing lately, the division over
civil rights. The old Dixiecrats are slipping one by one to the

Republican Party, or retiring and being replaced by new Republican faces. The new Southern leaders coming along are a moderate breed, much closer to the majority views in their party; there has been a great evolution from Orval Faubus to Dale Bumpers, or from Claude Kirk to Reubin Askew.

Voter registration drives in 1972 and better financing for the Presidential campaign were two clear gains that will carry forward to 1976. The national party was better off materially, as Richard Nixon began his second term, than it had been in years. The Democrats controlled Congress and an increased number of governorships. Whether from this base the party could reconstitute itself depends primarily on whether the antithetical elements in it can combine into the synthesis I spoke of at the start of this chapter. The traditional party leaders and labor will have to forgive and forget the rough handling they have suffered at the hands of the vital new people who had backed McCarthy or Kennedy in 1968 and McGovern in 1972. And the newcomers in turn will have to grow out of their youthful arrogance, recognize what is good about older Democrats like George Meany and Hubert Humphrey, and learn that politics means working as best you can with imperfect people in an imperfect world. And finally, both factions will have to make further adjustments to bring women and minorities into positions of real significance in making and executing policy. It is a tall order, but not impossible. The alternative is a future in which the minority Republican Party will hold the White House and enough power in Congress and on the state level to ensure that the nation's social problems continue to worsen, particularly the drift into two separate societies for blacks and whites. Meanwhile, the crumbling hulk of the Democratic Party will stagger from disaster to disaster, doing the country no good and making it harder to put together a new coalition through the vehicle of a third party.

XIV.

Looking Both Ways

WHEN I THINK over my campaign for President one thing seems marvelous—how much we accomplished with next to no money, with a haphazard, volunteer organization, and with no planning worthy of the name. We went a long distance on very little. The only way I can explain it is that there must have been a lot of people who were fed up with traditional candidates and campaigns and eager to throw themselves into an effort to change the way things are done and open up national politics to full participation by women, minorities and other excluded groups. Sometimes when I talk to people who were with me at Miami or in one of the state campaigns, they express the same wonder I feel—how far could we have gone if we had done it right? With professional organization and management in the national office, adequate financing and proper liaison with the enthusiastic volunteers we had in Massachusetts, California and a dozen other places, it seems well within the bounds of possibility that I would have had four hundred delegates or more going into the convention.

But that did not happen, and it is not my nature to dwell on "what ifs . . ." The greatest thing about the campaign were the hundreds of beautiful, courageous and concerned people who worked for me without pay and without much thanks. They achieved a prodigious amount considering the handicaps we faced in running a black female candidate, short of money and lacking experienced help. Many of them will stay in local, state and national politics, and they will make great contributions if they keep the energy and idealism they displayed while working for me.

Veterans of other Presidential campaigns probably would never believe how small my organization really was. In the national office, a cramped three-room suite in the old Dodge House, I had only three full-time staff members, and poorly paid ones at that. The rest of the work was done by a few part-time helpers and volunteers. There was no press secretary. There were no specialists on the delegate selection process. A well-thumbed copy of the Common Cause *Delegate Selection Handbook* told the staff nearly everything they knew. The mainstays of the office were a Princeton junior named Liz Cohen, a former women's rights and civil rights activist, Virginia Kerr, and a housewife and mother of seven, Lori Collier. They and the volunteers did it all—scheduling trips, manning the phone, liaison with state and local organizations, sending out buttons and literature, everything.

One of the most loyal volunteers was a white man who I think was in his fifties, and who had worked for many years with church missions in Puerto Rico. Alan Pinkernell wrote my office to volunteer for the campaign and got no reply. But he flew from Puerto Rico to Washington anyway and showed up at the campaign office wanting to work. We told him we had no money to pay the staff. "I know," he said. "I'll get a job dishwashing at night and work for you during the day." For the rest of the campaign, Alan typed campaign contribution cards, stuffed envelopes, ran the mimeograph machine and did all the dull chores of a political office. At the end he said, "Well, we didn't make it, so let's start organizing now for 1976." That kind of dedication is impossible to hire; it has to be a gift from the heart.

At the end of it all, I am convinced that we achieved, at least, one thing. Throughout the campaign the question that plagued me was "But are you a *serious* candidate?" Translation: "You would have to be crazy to think a black woman has any chance to be President." So I started out as a freak candidate, a kind of political sideshow. But I wound up in the main tent. Although I did not come very close to the nomination, I came closer than several of the white male candidates who, at the outset, were given a fair chance to make it all the way.

Sometimes I say that my campaign was an illustration of what Marshall McLuhan meant by "the medium is the message." The mere fact that a black woman dared to run for President, *seriously*, not expecting to win but sincerely trying to, is what it was all about. "It can be done"; that was what I was trying to say, by doing it.

It is important that I never made the rights of women or of blacks a primary theme of my campaign but insisted on making my role that of a potential voice for all the out-groups, those included. As best I could, I tried to keep stressing the principle that our government cannot keep on being primarily responsive to the privileged white upper classes but must serve the human needs of every citizen. Long unmet needs for housing, health care, pensions on which the aged can live decently, effective schools everywhere, including the poorest neighborhoods—all these and more cannot be neglected any longer, I kept saying. The human values must start to come first in government; people in need must be helped, not written off as malcontent, demanding, lazy, ignorant bums and cheats.

Our democracy remains immature, fundamentally retarded, as long as class, generational and race discrimination is perpetuated. The lethargic, bungling machinery of government is not working because it is the captive of powerful interests whose survival depends on keeping the system as unresponsive and unrepresentative as it is. My goal was to shake things up a little. I think I made a dent or two; time will tell.

At any rate, I feel the Chisholm candidacy accomplished one thing. The next time a woman of whatever color, or a dark-skinned person of whatever sex aspires to be President, the way should be a little smoother because I helped pave it. Perhaps some black or Spanish-speaking child already dreams of running for the Presidency someday, because a black woman has dared to. That child's dream would be more than enough for me to have accomplished, would it not? And is not that kind of dream a great gain for American society?

In terms of black politics, I think an effect of my campaign has been to increase the independence and self-reliance of many local elected black officials and black political activists from the domination of the political "superstars." What happened at Miami, when their interests were ignored, their wishes never determined and their votes treated as bargaining pawns by a handful of men who thought they were national black leaders, has left a profound impression. It was an educational experience for many blacks who realized that they were misled and exploited as badly by leaders of their own race as they ever had been by white politicians. An immediate result was the widespread lack of enthusiasm they felt for the McGovern campaign. But a more important, certainly more positive, outcome has been that they have started to challenge the dominance of many of the national figures whose leadership they once accepted, to their regret. This trend will certainly continue.

The United States was said not to be ready to elect a Catholic to the Presidency when Al Smith ran in the 1920s. But Smith's nomination may have helped pave the way for the successful campaign John F. Kennedy waged in 1960. Who can tell? What I hope most is that now there will be others who will feel themselves as capable of running for high political office as any wealthy, good-looking white male. Their way will still be hard, but it is essential that they travel it. We Americans have a chance to become someday a nation in which all racial stocks and classes can exist in their own selfhoods, but meet on a basis of respect and equality and live together, socially, economically and politically. We can become a dynamic equilibrium, a harmony of many very different elements, in which the whole will be greater than all its parts and greater than any society the world has seen before. It can still happen. I hope I did a little to make it happen. I am going to keep trying to make it happen as long as I am able. I will not run for President again, but in a broad sense my campaign will continue. In fact, it is just beginning.

Appendix A
Position Papers

Several of the position papers that were written and circulated during my campaign unfortunately continue to be as relevant, as I write this, as they were when they were issued in 1972, and I greatly fear they will keep their pertinence for several years to come. For that reason, and for what historic interest they might someday have, here are three of them in full, dealing with Africa, foreign aid and the American system of justice. Part of a fourth, on the economy, is also included.

Equality of Commitment–Africa

THIS ADMINISTRATION'S POLICY toward Africa, like that which it has followed toward its own black citizens, has been one of "benign neglect," if not simply plain neglect. The Nixon administration has ignored the tragic problems facing the poor nations of Black Africa. It has wiped out of its consciousness, if indeed such a notion ever existed there, the idea that the richest country in the world—Christian, young and revolutionary in origin—should be able, and is morally obligated, to help the Africans in their fight against ignorance and poverty.

This policy is therefore identical to that which has been followed toward Americans. Just as the Nixon administration has refused to allocate the resources necessary to help the poor in this country, so President Nixon has cut foreign aid to the lowest level in the history of the program, admitting that his 1969–70 program was the lowest aid recommendation proposal since the program began.

The spirit in which generous and useful economic aid programs for Africa were established and in which the Peace Corps was created in the early 1960s has, in fact, been replaced by a great moral vacuum, cynically filled only by another expensive and empty Vice Presidential junket to various African nations having authoritarian governments. In the meantime, we have watched as some Africans began to look elsewhere in recent years for the sympathy and help which we once gave them. An open and rather understandable public contempt for the American government has developed among Africans and other poor peoples of the world as a result of this government's attitude toward them.

Africa has, of course, been swept in and out of the vortex of cold war politics on numerous occasions. With Soviet interest in Africa apparently low for the moment, the Nixon administration has also decided to ignore the area, so long as it seems to be free from the threat of "Communist subversion." At home, the same attitude prevails—ignore the ghettos unless they blow up, and then send troops.

So, in the absence of a clear external threat to Africa, this administration has consistently pursued the same kind of callous, insensitive, and reactionary policy toward Black Africa that it has toward black Americans. It recently ignored, for example, United Nations economic sanctions against Rhodesia in order to permit the importation of Rhodesian chrome. It has refused to condemn in clear and categorical terms the white minority governments of Rhodesia, South Africa and Portugal. It has tolerated the insulting refusal of the South African regime to permit Arthur Ashe, one of the finest tennis players in the world, to play there. It has coldly ignored the struggling liberation movements in Angola, Mozambique, Zimbabwe and other places. It has no meaningful and systematic contact with the Organization of African Unity.

Yet, despite this policy, or nonpolicy, this administration is still capable of flying into a rage and sulking when African nations oppose us in the United Nations, as many did regarding the seating of China. In Africa as at home, we should clearly understand that the Nixon administration is a minority government, representing the wealthy and vested interests. As such, it is on the defensive, confronted by a coalition of not only the nonwhite minorities but any of their poor white people as well. This particular administration is distrusted because of the narrowness of its vision and rigidity of its attitudes toward the poor majority of the world's peoples. There should be no surprise, then, that the position of the United States in the United Nations and in the world at large has seriously eroded during the Nixon administration.

The racial attitudes of this administration are well known by blacks here and in Africa. The negative image of the character of this administration is shared by black Americans and black Africans. President Nixon has not only failed to bring this nation together, but he has, through his attitudes toward Africa, contributed to the racial and economic polarizations so great a threat to the entire international community. In so doing, this government has blithely permitted African-American relations to disintegrate to the lowest level in recent history, ignoring the blood relationship which binds so many Americans to Africa and oblivious of the consequences which are sure to come.

I wish to stress that I do not propose a huge giveaway program to Africa in the face of our enormous needs here at home, nor am I calling for worldwide revolution against the powers that be. I offer rather a new attitude of sympathetic solidarity with the poor in Africa and a policy which would include at least these key elements:

1. A fresh look at our relations with those European states maintaining racist policies in African countries, a review of our relations with each African nation, and the development of an understanding of the causes for which the various liberation groups in Africa are now fighting;

2. The appointment of highly qualified black Americans to top positions in the cabinet, the courts and the diplomatic service to let Africa and the world know that America is a multiracial nation and proud of it;

3. Preferential trade agreements with black African countries and support for reduced air fares between Africa and America;

4. Increased economic aid to Africa, to be administered by recognized and efficient international organizations, in close cooperation with the World Bank and International Monetary Fund;

5. The systematic condemnation in word and deed of the racist policies of white minority governments in Rhodesia, South Africa, Mozambique and Angola. With respect to South Africa and its barbarous system of apartheid, I would propose a ban on new American investment; a total ban on South African participation in international athletic events, abolition of the sugar quota. With specific respect to Portugal, I would propose a review of the need for our base in the Azores, followed by the expulsion of Portugal from NATO. With specific respect to Southern Rhodesia, I support all United Nations measures thus taken and I refuse to lend my support to such ludicrous so-called settlements as that to which Great Britain has just agreed;

6. A Presidential visit to those African countries struggling to develop progressive and liberal governments;

7. Finally, I intend to make known to Africans in every possible way that the government of the United States understands and sympathizes with them in their struggle against the terrible problems of tribalism, multiplicity of languages, lack of investment capital,

lack of jobs and lack of even minimal health and sanitary necessities.

We will help Africa as we are best able, and Africans will realize that compassion and respect for their humanity are once again the underlying attitudes behind American policy in Africa.

Foreign Aid

THE LEGISLATIVE DEBACLE that occurred in 1971 over the Foreign Aid bill has shown clearly that the American foreign aid program, in operation for twenty-five years, has reached the point where its future is in real doubt. Congress has appropriated less funds for the program than ever before. The reasons for the widespread discontent with the program are varied. Some argue that it has been a rat hole into which the U.S. has poured countless millions of dollars for nothing. Others argue that we have given aid to "Communist" or "leftist" governments who have used it against American interests.

The most serious criticism of foreign aid, however, is coming from those who have always staunchly supported aid. We are concerned that foreign aid seems to be failing to achieve its own prescribed objectives. We feel that our foreign aid is in fact retarding long-term growth abroad, including political development of the poor nations. For this reason, many of us have come to realize the necessity for a radically different approach. We are therefore not talking of abolishing foreign aid but of restructuring and revitalizing it.

We know that the gap between the rich and poor nations of the world is widening. We know that this gap increasingly threatens international stability. We have seen in the past decade internal uprisings and continuing domestic political and social turmoil in country after country in the developing world. Let us make no mistake about it—this is a historic period in international affairs. Throughout the developing world there is a revolution going on involving radical, structural change in the political, social and economic systems. It is in our interest, I suggest, and in the interest of humanity that this revolution be peaceful. The tragedy of our foreign aid program—and what has caused its near wreckage—is the fact that our foreign aid policy has for too long combined an offering of lip service to broad structural change with the systematic lending of actual support for the status quo. Under the guise of an unending, paranoiac anti-Communist crusade, we have shipped guns and napalm to self-serving and cynical dictators all over the world to use against those among their own countrymen who have tried to make real in their nations that which we have so piously declared we faithfully support everywhere—freedom, democracy and self-determination. Our foreign aid has too often provided a source of patronage and political strength for the existing power structure in poor nations. All over the world, it is American weapons and the assistance of U.S. military groups which repressive dictatorships have used, and are still using to stifle real reform.

Under the foreign aid program, the United States has become the chief arms supplier of mankind. Where we once proclaimed proudly that America was the "Arsenal of Democracy," we have become in the eyes of many the "Arsenal of Reactionary Violence" on the international scene. Having devoted relatively so little to the effort overseas, we have repeatedly intervened, as in Vietnam and as in the Dominican Republic in 1965, to prop up repressive or incompetent regimes confronted with the explosive discontent of their own peoples. Instead of providing sufficient sums of aid to poor countries to help them build roads, provide electric power and improve education, we have rushed tanks, airplanes, guns, bombs and military advisers to such reactionary governments as those in Spain, Brazil, Portugal, Greece and Cambodia. Since 1959, for example, Portugal has received nearly $400 million in American aid under NATO—and used a large part of it in Black Africa to repress liberation movements seeking political self-determination. This has been a clear violation of NATO treaty terms. In Greece, our aid has only served to create the impression among countless Greeks that we are single-handedly upholding a government which has imposed and maintained martial law on its people for over four years, with no prospects for a return to constitutional democracy.

Why is it that we are always shipping murderous weapons to dictatorships to repress their poor and dispossessed? Why shouldn't we be sending economic aid to benefit the poor and to help eradicate those conditions which cause their discontent in the first place?

The United States is the richest country in the world, yet our foreign aid has decreased to the point where, under the Nixon administration, it has reached the lowest level ever. Among the sixteen members of the Development Assistance Committee, formed in 1961 under U.S. leadership, America ranked thirteenth among the wealthy nations in terms of its public and private foreign aid disbursements when measured as a percent of the gross national product. Today in Latin America, the social revolution is under way with elements of the church, universities and trade unions pushing for reform in their countries. Yet, the Nixon administration has gutted the Alliance for Progress and the Peace Corps—two imaginative programs that so favorably impressed people everywhere not so long ago as products of the youthful idealism which America once symbolized. In the last few years, in Latin America, Americans have been kidnapped and assassinated, a once close ally has freely elected a Marxist government, and other countries have nationalized American companies operating there.

The foreign aid program has become too tied up with the supply of guns, rather than butter, to continue to serve its original, lofty purposes. It has become too often a political tool with which ambassadors could curry favor with the governments to which they are accredited. It has led America, a self-professed revolutionary nation, to become identified as a part of that bulwark of resistance to the profound changes now sweeping the Third World. We have given much aid—but too often of the wrong type and to the wrong governments—and that is why the foreign aid program is self-defeating and therefore no longer acceptable.

A new approach to foreign aid must be based on the premise that it is not only right for those of us who have to help those who have not, but that we ignore the frustrations of poverty at home and abroad at our own risk. We must create among the poor everywhere new confidence in our desire to help, rather than hinder, this contemporary demand for social justice. We must work to reduce hunger, disease, ignorance and poverty with the ultimate goal of higher living standards, more open and liberal societies and a stronger world community.

In so doing, we will prove that this great nation is in step with one of the great movements of history, and that it truly believes in the need to turn our swords into plowshares.

Economic and social development abroad is not something that can be precisely measured or that will be peaceful or even always consistent with our perceived interests. Substantial progress is being made in many countries. Aid is not obsolete or a boondoggle or a giveaway, and economic aid is no longer a political orphan. Those of us who support reduced military aid and greater economic aid abroad will continue to speak out for a more sophisticated and objective view of aid. If we wish the world to be secure and prosperous, as I am sure we all do, we must show a common concern for the common problems of all people. By so doing we will demonstrate that international leadership is a matter of performance and imagination rather than of arm twisting and distribution of largesse. We must provide a clear and confident commitment to the future, rather than the past, and I propose such initial steps as the following, many of which have been proposed by experts, to reshape our foreign aid program:

1. Greatly increased economic aid (to amount to 1 percent of the total U.S. GNP) to assist the poor countries in their struggle against ignorance and poverty;

2. Greatly decreased military aid abroad, including elimination of aid to repressive regimes such as those in Spain, Greece, Portugal and Cambodia;

3. Gradual abolition of the Agency for International Development and elimination of the American ambassadors' responsibility for the administration of U.S. assistance programs;

4. Increased multi-lateralization of aid through strengthened international and regional agencies including the

World Bank, the International Development Association, the Inter-American Development Bank and Regional Development Banks;

5. The opening of the developed countries' markets to exports from developing countries by the creation of an open, nondiscriminatory preference system featuring reduced tariffs and reduced excise taxes on imports from poor countries, with an immediate reduction of duties on Latin American goods exported to the United States;

6. Focusing of technical assistance on family planning, agriculture, education and vocational training;

7. Maximum funding for development loans;

8. The absence of paternalism or expectations of immediate economic or political reward;

9. Two years' authorization for aid funds rather than annual authorization in order to save Congress time and to provide greater time to organize and implement approved programs.

Justice in America

**Gun Control, Drug Abuse, Court, Police,
Prison Reform, Political and Civil Dissent**

IT IS IN the field of civil rights and criminal justice, or what the President calls "law and order," that the Nixon administration must be most severely condemned. This administration has virtually declared war on blacks, nonwhites and the young in this vitally sensitive area. The fundamental rights guaranteed to all Americans by the Constitution have too often been flagrantly and willfully ignored in the Nixon administration's discriminatory and repressive approach to criminal justice and civil liberties. This administration has talked a lot about law and order, but its blatantly political and partisan administration of justice is, in effect, undermining American democracy while real crime of all types continues to rise.

There is no question that crime is a valid and burning issue today. Crime crosses all social and economic boundaries, whether in the manifestation of violence or in the fear of its eventuality. America today is a nation barricaded into safety. Americans are fleeing to the suburbs, restaurant business activity is down during evening hours, and bus companies have fewer riders at night. Burglar alarm sales are up 40 to 60 percent over last year in Los Angeles. There are now more private police than public police, with the number of private police and security guards rising to approximately 800,000. The Library of Congress, lying in the shadow of the dome of the Capitol, has had to change its working hours so that the majority of its 4,000 employees can begin the journey homeward before the sun goes down.

Of every 10,000 women, seven are raped but 4,300 fear they might be. While the problem of crime preys particularly on the ghetto dweller, it has now invaded America's suburbs and rural areas as well.

The President who came to power in 1968 on a "law and order" platform has completely failed to halt the rise in crime, while simultaneously adopting various police-state tactics and methods whose constitutionality is in real doubt. The lack of positive leadership in fighting crime becomes clear when one looks at the sins of omission of this administration in moving against the sources of serious crime.

The President has given no meaningful support to the effort to control the open sale of guns, whose easy availability is unquestionably responsible for so many of the violent crimes committed today. He has procrastinated and then acted with too little, too late to halt the increase in drug abuse until it has risen to epidemic proportions. He has failed to generate prompt and sweeping reform of our 200-year-old prison system, which everyone now recognizes to be a monstrous failure with no pretense of rehabilitative treatment. He has failed to achieve meaningful reform of our courts, which too often violate standards of fairness, due process and common justice. He has ignored the recommendations of experts from his own crime commissions to reduce the number of acts considered crimes, thereby freeing the police for serious police work. He has refused to support efforts throughout the country to eliminate police corruption and brutality.

Of perhaps even greater seriousness are the sins of commission of the Nixon administration and law enforcement agencies throughout the nation during the last four years, actions and policies which have not only failed to halt the increase in crime but which are leading to a severe curtailment of freedom for all Americans. The Nixon administration has encouraged an institutionalized counterviolence which has given the green light to every local law enforcement or vigilante group in the country to act as it wishes in the execution of its perceived tasks.

Moreover, the administration has politicized this nation's Justice Department. The powers of the government have been too often marshaled, not against the actual criminals in the nation, but against those who oppose this administration politically. The harassment of newsmen who dare to criticize administration policies; expanded wiretapping, room-bugging and surveillance of the poor and black and even those attending Earth Day ceremonies; governmental overkill in the press, the courtroom—all represent a conscious and deliberate drive to encourage adjustment to the reality of life in "Nixon's America" rather than stimulating a creative means of changing some of the intolerable unfairness and inequities which still trouble the nation.

In its broad retreat on civil rights enforcement, in its attempt to place on the Supreme Court of the land men with records of such negative racial attitudes or juridical incompetence that members of the President's own party have felt compelled to vote against them, the Nixon administration has provoked widespread shock and dismay among millions of Americans that their government has become an "enemy" to its own people.

The demonstrable failure of the Nixon administration to effectively reduce crime lies in the fact that the President has chosen to neglect the miserable conditions in which crime is born and festers. Instead of attacking causes rather than symptoms, the administration has encouraged response to violence by counter-violence and a policy of instant justice.

During the last three years we have seen a proliferation of bloody raids with the killing of unarmed students at Kent State and Jackson State; the brutal and insane slaughter of prisoners and guards alike at Attica; and mass, unlawful arrests in the nation's capital last May Day.

The Nixon administration's preference for repression and persecution of political dissenters has taken greater precedence than court, police and prison reform. The record suggests that the administration's appalling lack of concern for the rights of the individual is exceeded only by its deeply ingrained authoritarian and reactionary instincts, fearful and dangerous perhaps because it rests on such a narrow basis of electoral support.

Let us look at the details of this record.

No Gun Control

The nation's chiefs of police have appealed for urgent efforts to control the sale of guns in this country. Private guns have caused more American deaths since the turn of the century than wars have caused since the beginning of the nation. America today has the highest gun accident rate in the world. Three beloved American leaders have been murdered in recent years by men who should never have been able to obtain the guns that fired the fatal bullets. Such an obvious link to crime cries out for attention, and I am baffled by the President's seeming indifference to this life-and-death issue.

Drug Abuse Out of Control

It has been said that 95 percent of the women incarcerated in the District of Columbia correctional institutions are drug addicts. Estimates of drug-related crimes in New York City run above 50 percent. For the past three years, the Nixon administration virtually ignored the scope of the drug problem—as long as its major effect appeared to be only on the poor and minorities. The Drug Abuse and Education Act of 1969, sponsored by 85 members of Congress, passed the House by a vote of 294 to 0, in spite of the administration's statement that the bill was "unnecessary."

The President later admitted that he thought the drug-abuse problem could be remedied by stiffening the penalties, but that he had a change of heart when it became clear that "the problem is not confined to a particular segment of society, but one which has begun to reach the upper middle classes." In other words, as long as the problem of drug abuse did not affect the children of the upper middle classes, stiff penalties and punishment would be his only answer to the problem.

Similarly, the President waited until the epidemic of heroin addiction among American servicemen in Vietnam was revealed to the public before he wheeled out his version of a crash program to counter it. This action came almost a year after a Senate subcommittee issued warnings that an epidemic was growing rapidly in the armed services, and the President later contradictorily announced a hiring freeze for staff in drug rehabilitation centers in Veterans' Administration hospitals.

Moreover, the Nixon administration has consistently hampered Congressional initiatives in the fight against drugs during the last three years. It has opposed legislation to establish a National Institute on Drug Abuse and Drug Dependence to coordinate existing programs and agencies. It has opposed Title I (National Institute on Drug Abuse) of the comprehensive Drug Abuse Prevention and Control Act, even though it was sponsored by the entire Labor and Public Welfare Committee of the Senate. It opposed greater controls on amphetamines, over half of whose production reaches illegal channels. It opposed the Senate amendments to the Economic Opportunity Act for community drug and alcoholism programs.

Even though 60 to 70 percent of the nation's communities have expressed interest in funding for drug programs, the administration offered no plans to assist with new community projects to lease drug treatment facilities; no plans to assist new community projects to build drug treatment facilities; no plans to fund more than four initiation and development grants for treatment and rehabilitation facilities for the entire country, and no plans to fund more than a few new education, research and training projects in drugs. The administration's incredible lack of leadership in this critical field has made far more difficult the efforts of those of us who are determined to eliminate this major source of crime and human misery, once and for all.

No Prison Reform

In the past three years, riots have broken out in New York's Tombs Prison, San Quentin, Attica, the Indiana Reformatory and elsewhere as inmates protested the cruel and degrading conditions of America's dungeons. Many experts have long attacked the punitive basis of our prison system, which has succeeded only in bringing out the worst in men and assuring their lifelong careers as criminals. The President's own Crime Commission, describing the system, found "overwhelming evidence of institutional shortcomings" in almost every part of the United States. New York's Joint Legislative Committee on Crime reported that one-fourth of all inmates in the state prisons believe "with reason" that they are victims of a "mindless, undirected and corrupt" system of criminal justice.

The 1972 budget for the Federal Bureau of Prisons calls for $189.7 million—an increase of only $66 million over the 1971 budget. Most of the increase, unfortunately, simply goes for new buildings and facilities. The Legal Enforcement Assistance Administration administrator, Richard W. Velde, estimates that a modern prison building program could cost $15 billion. The LEAA fiscal 1972 budget for corrections showed $97.5 million, but this money was allocated to the states in block grants over which the LEAA has little or no control. There is no federal guarantee that this money will be used as hoped. The prison system in America today remains a tragic failure and waste of money, and the prisons themselves remain reserved for those with dark skins, little money, and different life styles.

No Court Reform

No amount of money spent to reform prisons nor any program of inmate rehabilitation, no matter how carefully conceived, would be effective without an essential restructuring of our chaotic court system. The Nixon administration had vowed to reform the system. Chief Justice Warren Burger has called for major overhaul of the courts, as have many, yet the Nixon administration has again taken virtually no action to make the tools available. Its tinkering has been largely ineffectual and has not changed the fact that for those who are poor, powerless and nonwhite, sentencing is too often grossly disparate, illogical and unprincipled. Excessive bail continues to be the norm for these people.

With administration encouragement, the courts have developed mass production procedures in routine criminal cases, making a mockery of the trial process. Plea bargaining now receives full judicial approval. Administrative inefficiency and judicial or prosecutorial incompetence continue to create pressures in which defendants and society can only come out losers. The Chief Judge of the District of Columbia

Superior Court has been moved to describe the courts as "factories where defendants are quickly processed like so many sausages." Instant justice has become the hallmark of the Nixon justice, with overcrowded courts dispensing assembly-line justice.

The danger in the present criminal justice system is that it is cynical and unfair to blacks and other minorities, including migrant workers. The law appears to be an instrument of oppression; to the poor, a barrier to alleviation of an unjust status quo; to the young, a coercer of conformity to middle-class, puritan virtues. Most of us recognize that there are gross inequities in the American criminal justice system, a system which guarantees the second-class status of minorities and poor people, combats differing life styles, and silences those who might challenge the status quo.

One seldom hears these days about the prosecution of business leaders for such widespread and socially harmful crimes as deceptive advertising, pollution, selling dangerous merchandise and violating anti-trust laws. Real estate agents are rarely prosecuted for blockbusting or practicing illegal racial discrimination in renting and selling. Election laws limiting political campaign contributions are violated regularly every two and four years, and there are no enforcement policies. Where are the prosecutions of white-collar criminals committing crimes of falsification, fraud, libel, bribery, health code violations, perjury, income-tax evasion and price fixing? Where are the convictions of slumlords, polluters and those who make unsafe autos? To these people of "respectable" background go the written warnings and mild penalties.

The New York Joint Legislative Committee revealed that several thousand arrests of organized crime figures in the last decade had resulted in prison sentences in only 5 percent of the cases. A class nature of law enforcement process continues to exist under the Nixon administration, functioning to maintain a racist relationship between the white majority and the black, brown, red and yellow minorities. Not only do the powerful manage by and large to escape the sanctions of the criminal justice system, but they also manipulate the system for their own political ends. Thus, James R. Hoffa is given a Presidential pardon while others, nonwhite and less influential, are passed over.

Laws forbidding armed robbery and burglary have a very different impact for a millionaire and for an unemployed young black male in a ghetto where the unemployment rate is 25 percent. The evil of racism and the indignities of second-class citizenship still characterize America's system of criminal justice, the power of the purse appears to remain decisive to an administration manifesting thinly concealed contempt for the racial minorities, the poor and the young who remain disproportionately victimized by law enforcement.

No Police Reform

Rampaging police brutality and summary justice in the black community, and evidence of widespread police corruption, as in New York, have for too long characterized police work. Excessive police violence, discriminatory treatment of Chicano juveniles, biased enforcement of motor vehicle regulations, racial discourtesies, the excessive use of "stop and frisk" laws are all various forms of police harassment and intimidation common to the poor and nonwhite communities. Vigilante squads and right-wing political repression have sprouted from coast to coast.

The administration has shown its lack of concern for this intolerable abuse of police power by simply giving more arms to police forces and by promoting Orwellian police tactics such as "No-Knock," which strikes at the fundamental right of every American to be secure in his home. No meaningful federal assistance has been offered for minority hiring or significant increases in salaries, which would help draw better police personnel. Not unexpectedly, the Law Enforcement Assistance Administration, the Justice Department's liaison with local police forces, has been charged with a "grossly inadequate" civil rights performance by the U.S. Civil Rights Commission, in connection with its legal responsibilities in this area.

Blocking Civil Rights Progress

In adopting the "Southern Strategy," the Nixon administration served notice that it would systematically eliminate the government's crucial role in ensuring the civil rights of all Americans. It has not only said nothing when black schoolchildren's buses were burned or black votes thrown away. It has instead spoken out to strike governmental political opposition to school busing and adopt a policy of refusal to enforce civil rights statutes, particularly in the fields of employment, housing, education, agricultural services, labor programs, public accommodations and public facilities.

The record is clear. This administration has moved to wipe out the effectiveness of the legal services program, a part of the Office of Economic Opportunity. The Attorney General failed to use the powers accorded him by the 1970 Voting Rights Act and allowed a discriminatory new voting law to go into effect in Mississippi. In twenty counties, the registration rolls were wiped clean, and registrants were told to reregister. This meant that over six years of registration efforts were wiped off the books. The Federal District Court in Biloxi, Mississippi, reviewed the law and stated that it failed to meet the burden of proof in court, and criticized the Attorney General for taking an "obtuse" illegal course in the enforcement of federal voting laws.

In May, 1971, the House Judiciary Subcommittee on Civil Rights accused the Nixon administration of inadequate enforcement of federal voting laws and inviting "irresponsible" people to disregard them. The Attorney General was charged to set an example for the country for obedience to the law, rather than complain about existing law.

Civil rights lawyers have quit this administration en masse, and a suit was filed in district court by civil rights attorneys, charging the Attorney General and Assistant Attorney General with failure to enforce the laws.

In short, the cause of civil rights and human rights has been systematically jeopardized by the Nixon administration. The "Southern Strategy" has opened the door to the past, as shown in the recent (1972) statewide elections in Mississippi where intimidation of black voters and the ignoring of black votes once again undercut American democracy.

Crushing of Political Dissent

Under the Nixon administration, America has entered a new phase of political repression against the activist forces struggling for change. While crime ravages our cities, a policy of overt political reaction and the expansion of police power have been given top priority by this administration. Spying is out of control, with the Army at one point spying on Senators, the proliferation of FBI wiretaps and bugs, revelations of networks of paid informers, and the political persecution of the Chicago 7, the Berrigans, Angela Davis and Daniel Ellsberg.

America has entered the road to 1984, with the President politicizing a Justice Department bent on restricting individual liberties and monitoring the lives of countless Americans.

The Nixon administration has devoted its efforts to crushing political opposition with the result that force, intimidation and repression are undermining our democracy, rather than ensuring an orderly society in which human dignity can flourish. Many of the hack politicians in the Justice Department appear to be men who see order as the rigid freezing into place of the America they have made and who think law has no higher function than to preserve that order.

I am terribly concerned about crime in America. I believe that the abatement of crime lies not in police hands, but in reducing the stresses and strains which produce, in some, disrespect for the law, and in others, a sense of grievance expressing itself in violence and crime. Criminal justice is dependent upon and largely derives from social justice. The only solution for the problem of class and race bias in the courtroom or by the police and correctional systems is the eradication of bias from American life—we must do away with oppressive functions and with social prejudices and inequities to significantly reduce crime.

The Nixon criminal justice approach is adding to the increasingly dangerous polarization of conflict in America. Instead of strengthening the belief in the legitimacy of authority, it has generated cynicism and bitterness. Our entire society will inevitably suffer from this blindness in our national leadership. While working for social justice throughout the nation, I propose the following steps as a beginning for reform of our criminal justice system and the reduction of crime:

1. Federal prohibition of handguns, strict licensing and registration of all other weapons;

2. Appointment of more blacks, nonwhites, and women as judges and wardens, to the FBI, police forces and all law enforcement agencies, and as parole board members, probation officers, minority prison guards, etc.

3. FBI reform by giving the FBI greater responsibilities in civil rights enforcement and combating white-collar crime, including organized crime;

4. Prison reform, including open visitation, creation of programs to allow prisoners to obtain college degrees, and a bill of rights for prisoners to include:
   a. *freedom of threat from physical abuse;*
   b. *freedom of worship;*
   c. *unrestricted access to legal assistance;*

5. The creation of special courts or judges for alcoholism, petty larceny, and civilian review boards for police corruption;

6. Greater financial support for local and state police with emphasis on attracting higher grades of personnel into police work;

7. Beefing up local and federal anti-crime efforts with the sharing of information in order to allow a coordinated attack on organized crime in all areas, especially in drug traffic;

8. Full support for the U.S. Civil Rights Commission and a non-political Justice Department;

9. Applying criminal laws uniformly;

10. Doing away with indeterminate sentencing and minimizing discretionary powers of police, judges and other judicial functionaries;

11. Separation of treatment and punishment, making therapy and counseling available to all prisoners on a truly voluntary basis;

12. Greater enforcement of anti-trust laws.

The Economy

(AFTER A LONG analysis, here omitted, of the failures of the Nixon administration on the economic front, I offered eight proposals as alternatives. This is the pertinent section of that paper.)

No administration can be so indissolubly connected to the interests of big business and special interests, and still work to eliminate its crisis of credibility and intent among millions of Americans.

I believe that the future of our great society depends upon the ending of government by the conservative, repressive and selfish. It depends upon the ending of the economic exploitation of the common man, black and white, by those privileged powers which now rule Washington.

My administration will move emphatically to assist those Americans presently estranged from the American economic system. It will seek representation for those performing vital services, such as domestic workers, while gaining miserable compensation. It will devote itself to the creation of a more balanced economy and to the final elimination of the intolerable inequality and poverty which we should all be ashamed to admit exist in this, the wealthiest nation in the history of man. Some of the principal means which I support toward these ends are as follows:

1. Ending the billion-dollar cost of U.S. military involvement in Indochina.

2. Creation of a federal family assistance program to replace the present welfare program and the food stamp program, which is a failure. The initial minimum guaranteed income for a family of four would be $6,400.

3. Tax Reform. The tax proposals of the Nixon administration have consistently favored business over the low-income consumer. State, local and city taxes are increasing while the progressive, graduated income tax has been reduced. My tax reform program will reduce unfairness and special privilege in the following ways:
   a. *Increased individual and corporate income tax (even a 1 percent increase would raise $6 billion);*
   b. *Elimination of the oil depletion allowance;*
   c. *Elimination of the capital gains tax;*
   d. *Elimination of regressive federal payroll taxes;*
   e. *Establishing of excess profits tax;*

4. Reductions in federal spending:

   f. Elimination of the huge federal subsidies paid to rich farmers not to grow crops;

   g. Reduced spending on federal highway construction;

   h. Reduced defense spending; including the closing of unnecessary military installations and the reduction of our troop levels abroad by 50 percent;

   i. Reduced spending on space programs and cancellation of the space shuttle project;

5. Expansion of job opportunities through creation of 500,000 useful public service jobs, with preference to the 350,000 unemployed veterans. Greater federal assistance for labor manpower training programs. Increased federal programs to put highly skilled unemployed engineers to work in mass transit, air and water pollution control programs; maintenance of some form of wage-price controls, particularly on rents.

6. Federal legislation to guarantee equal opportunities for women in attaining jobs, equal pay and promotions.

7. Creation of a comprehensive national day care system to permit more mothers to work.

8. Greater federal support for O.E.O., E.E.O.C., O.M.B.E. and S.B.A—greater support for minority enterprise and employment.

Appendix B

Campaign Speeches

Most of my campaign speeches were ad lib, and if any of them survive, it must be in the form of films or tape. The topics they covered are all dealt with in the body of the book. But there are two set speeches on special topics that I used during the period of late 1971 and early 1972 that, like the position papers in Appendix A, still have an unhappy relevance and are likely to continue to have. The first, freely adapted to suit the occasion, I have given before a number of women's groups. The second was given originally at a hospital administrators' meeting in Philadelphia.

Economic Justice for Women

AT ONE TIME or another we have all used the phrase "economic justice." This afternoon I would like to turn your attention to economic justice for women. Of course this is only an illusory phrase, as it is an undeniable fact that economic justice for American women does not exist.

As I look back over the years of my own lifetime, the transformation in the economic, social and political role we women play in American life has been almost incredible. But we are still quite a long way from anything like equality of opportunity. We are still in a highly disadvantaged position relative to men. This is revealed by our earnings. On the average, women who are full-time, year-round workers receive only about 60 percent of what men who are similarly employed earn. The median income for full-time, year-round women workers was $3,973, compared to $6,848 for men. This is somewhat below the official poverty level decreed for a family of four. This reflects the fact that we are all too often paid less for doing the same work; even more it reflects our concentration in the lower-paid, lesser-skilled occupations, and we are steadily losing ground.

Columnist Clayton Fritchey, in "Women in the Office," noted that, "although more women are working, their salaries keep falling behind men's. Some occupations are still closed, by law, to women. In 1940 women held 45 percent of all professional and technical positions as against 37 percent today." Among all employed women—not college women alone—82 percent are clerical, sales, factory and farmworkers or in service occupations. Six percent of us are teachers in the grammar and high schools and only 7 percent of us are medical and health workers, college teachers or other professional and technical workers. Just 5 percent of us are managers, officials or proprietors.

The factors that have narrowed our opportunities are multiple and complex. There are restrictive hiring practices. There is discrimination in promotions. Many myths, which run entirely counter to the facts, maintain that women make poor supervisors, or that they have substantially higher rates of absenteeism and labor turnover. A recent Department of Labor survey revealed that women are more reliable and are absent less frequently than the male population of our labor force. The myth about the unreliability of women is somewhat like the one about women being bad drivers. That one has been disproven lately also by the insurance companies—women pay lower rates.

The claim is often made, and without the slightest justification, that even women with more than adequate training and knowledge lack the ability to assume higher-level positions in industry. As the late President Kennedy declared in December, 1961, in the opening words of his executive order establishing a Commission on the Status of Women, "These continuing prejudices and outmoded customs act as barriers to the full realization of women's basic rights, which should be respected and fostered as part of our nation's commitment to human dignity, freedom and democracy." When President Nixon's first nomination for the Supreme Court was rejected, it appalled and disturbed me greatly that he did not even consider nominating a woman. Our women have too long been overlooked for positions of importance in policy-making and decision areas.

The under-utilization of American women is one of the most senseless wastes of this century. It is a waste our country can no longer afford. David Deith, a financial reporter, wrote that the Swedish national income could be 25 percent higher if women's labor potential was fully utilized. The standard of living in France would rise 35 percent if women were as professionally active as men. To my knowledge no comparable studies have been made in the U.S. on women, but Federal Reserve Board member Andrew Brimmer once estimated that racial bias costs our nation $20 billion a year and there are five times more women in America than there are blacks.

Meeting the challenge presented by a dynamic, expanding

economy in the 1970s and beyond will require that American business employ all the financial, material and human resources at its command. We are expected to maintain and improve a high standard of living for a rapidly growing population. We are called upon to meet greater demands for American goods abroad.

The greatest domestic problems of today—poverty in our urban ghettos, inadequate housing, substandard housing, the lack of meaningful, rewarding jobs for many thousands of our citizens—are all challenges that the business sector is being asked to take up. At the same time, we must maintain a growing economy in which all can participate.

In mobilizing our resources for the task, we must make sure that none are overlooked; particularly we must train, develop and use effectively the knowledge and skills of all our people. It is not enough that we talk of the nation's manpower needs; we are going to need "womanpower" as well.

Statistically, the simple, inevitable fact is that America will have to draw upon the whole of her human resources and offer vastly wider opportunities, without discrimination in race or sex, if we are to accomplish these objectives.

The male prejudice against female achievement is usually in a subtle, often unconscious form. Men who would recoil in horror at the thought of being called anti-feminist, who view themselves as impartial, feel no inconsistency in saying the "little woman's" place is in the kitchen, with the kids, etc., etc. When these men are accused of prejudice, they reply that they are being sensitive to the "female character."

When I decided to run for Congress, I knew I would encounter both anti-black and anti-feminist sentiments. What surprised me was the much greater virulence of the sex discrimination. It seems that while many, many Americans still harbor racist emotions, they are no longer based on so-called racial characteristics. Paternalism has to a great extent disappeared from racial bias. But I was constantly bombarded by both men and women exclaiming that I should return to teaching, a woman's vocation, and leave politics to the men.

Like every other form of discrimination, anti-feminism is destructive both to those who perpetrate it and to its victims. Male school-teachers, for example, are well aware of this. They have had to fight against both men and women who cast aspersions on their maleness because of their vocation. No one knows how many men have declined careers in teaching jobs they would have enjoyed because of the "female" character of that profession. When one group of society is as oppressed as American women are, no one can be free. Males, with their anti-feminism, maim both themselves and their women.

Like black people, women have had it with this bias. We are no longer content to trade off our minds and abilities in exchange for having doors opened for us by gallant men. While most men laugh jeeringly at the fledgling "women's liberation groups" springing up across the nation, they should know that countless women—including their cohorts, their wives and their daughters—silently applaud such groups. We—American women—are beginning to respond to our oppression. While most of us are not yet revolutionaries, we are getting in tune with the cry of the liberation groups. Women are not inherently passive or peaceful; we're not inherently anything but human. And like every other oppressed people rising today, we're out for freedom—by any means necessary.

Such is the predicament of all American women; the problem is multiplied for those of us who operate also under racial prejudice. So far most of the feminine revolution has been directed at the problems of professional women whose skills are not recognized or rewarded. However, this very fact that professional ladies have spokesmen who will protest their condition gives them hope of alleviating their suffering. I turn now to the specific dilemma of the black woman.

The feminine revolution has been headed mostly by middle-class white professional women and aimed toward the higher-level jobs. More of our attention should be directed toward those women who comprise the menial working force of our country. Particularly, the black woman, who usually has to find employment as a maid, housekeeper, day worker, cafeteria helper, etc. These are dead-end jobs, jobs inherently degrading and humiliating, jobs which barely provide a subsistence existence. Today young women are revolting against this kind of subservient employment. They refuse to take a job which robs them of their self-respect and dignity in exchange for a few dollars.

They want the opportunity to prove their worth, to show, to both whites and black men, that they are women, black women, and that they are proud.

Most of these black women lack the academic training to compete for professional and white-collar jobs. Our society must begin to give them training. But in the meantime, there are definite steps which can be taken now to utilize the talents of black women and to provide them with an income above the poverty line, steps which will eliminate the discrimination on the basis of race and sex.

Some of you may be thinking, "How can she say that this discrimination is so virulent? Isn't she the first black female member of Congress? That proves that the bias isn't really too great." On the contrary, my battle was long, incredibly hard and continual. Because I pushed, I encountered the strongest prejudice of less competent males, both black and white. That I won is a tribute to the women in my neighborhood who are finally saying no to the system. They are fed up. And as each day goes by and the awareness of women to our plight grows, there will be more and more women who will say no.

We live in revolutionary times. The shackles that various groups have worn for centuries are being cast off. This is evidenced by the"developing" nations of the world, which we consider, for the most part, underdeveloped. Countries such as India, Ceylon (Sri Lanka) and Israel have women for Prime Ministers and in other decision-making positions.

American women must stand and fight—be militant even— for rights which are ours. Not necessarily on soapboxes should we voice our sentiments, but in the community and at the polls. We must demand and get day care centers, better job training, more opportunities to enter fields and professions of our choosing and stop accepting what is handed to us.

The Cost of Care

LAST JANUARY, WHEN the 92nd Congress convened, there was high hope in some quarters that at last action was coming to make medical care available to all our citizens. Our health system, never adequate, had broken under the load of a rising population, endless inflation and changing patterns of life. Millions of Americans had no doctor to turn to when they became ill or injured, and millions more could not afford to go to a doctor if one was available. There are abundant statistics to show the effect—those on infant mortality are perhaps the most striking. The richest nation in history was unable to provide even emergency medical care for all its citizens, to say nothing of services that would keep them healthy. Public pressure was becoming intense. Something had to be done.

But nothing was done, and nothing has been done yet. President Nixon has introduced a health care plan. Senator Edward Kennedy has proposed one that was designed by the AFL-CIO. The insurance industry, the American Medical

Association and several other interests have designed their own plans. All are before the appropriate committees of Congress. In the House, there have been extensive hearings.

But whether there will be any action next year, amid the pressures and jealousies of a Presidential election campaign, is a very serious question. Since the need is so great, we must be hopeful, and I am going to assume today that Congress will pass some kind of a bill to alleviate the scandalous shortcomings of our national health system. What I want to go on to do is to discuss the major proposals that have been made and explain why I feel that none of them, nor any combination of them, will greatly improve the system.

Comprehensive, elaborate and revolutionary as some of the health system reform proposals seem, they are all in fact little more than "quick-fix" schemes—merely tinkering with the system. All of them are basically efforts to make it possible for more people to afford medical care. Health is still a commodity that will be bought and sold, under any of the reform schemes. People must still pay, one way or another, for the services that will keep them alive and well.

Medicare and Medicaid have demonstrated, I would think, the folly of approaching the problem purely by a scheme for paying the bills. The two old-age health systems have procured more services for some people, but at enormous cost—not direct cost as much as indirect. The availability of the federal payments has driven fees, drug prices and, above all, hospital and nursing home costs, sky-high. The result is that they are now priced beyond the reach of many persons who once could afford them. Dumping huge amounts of money into our present health services delivery system will have the same effect. It will not work, whether it is done through a national health insurance scheme or one to subsidize private insurance. It will be Medicaid all over again—squared or cubed.

According to one analysis, the problem with Medicaid was that it mushroomed the *demand* for medical services while the *supply* stayed more or less constant. The result was that prices were driven up. Looking at it another way, the proprietors of the limited supply of health resources saw a bonanza in the new federal checks and responded to the opportunity by charging all that the traffic would bear. A solution has been offered out of classical economic theory: increase the supply to meet the demand. President Nixon's health plan, which is otherwise a strange patchwork of proposals, is probably stronger in this respect than any of the others. It includes authorization for new aid plans for training health professionals, and it has a promising idea for experimenting with ways to make more efficient use of the limited supply of experts we have, the health maintenance organization. An H-M-O is, as you probably know, basically a group practice by several physicians, supported by a staff of paraprofessional persons—nurses, laboratory technicians and so forth—and nonmedical aides. This is a first-rate suggestion in some ways, and I must confess that its inclusion in the administration plan surprised those of us who had been expecting the White House to labor and produce a mouse of a modest health insurance-subsidy scheme.

The elaborate national insurance plan developed by the AFL-CIO and backed by Senator Edward Kennedy and Representative Martha Griffiths would, if it worked, apparently mean that no American would ever have to pay a doctor or hospital bill again—except for some dental, psychiatric and extended-care patients. Its fiscal soundness has been doubted, but I am sure that it could be reworked to make it fiscally possible, if it is not already. But neither the Nixon plan nor the Kennedy plan, nor any of the others, offers a really sound solution to our national health care crisis.

Why are our health services not meeting the needs of the great majority of Americans? The citizens' board of inquiry into health services for Americans has found some very basic reasons. Let me enumerate seven of them, and show how none of the health system reform proposals now under consideration would meet the need.

First, the board found that Americans go to a doctor or a hospital, generally, only when sickness or injury makes it absolutely necessary. One main reason is that they cannot afford medical service for minor problems, or even for major ones that do not seem at the moment to be disabling or threaten to be fatal. A national health insurance system would, if it worked, remove the problem of payment— although, as I have just discussed, it would be almost certain to do so at the cost of accelerating the already ruinous inflation in the price of health care. But a universal insurance scheme would do little, if anything, about medicine's preoccupation with corrective, rather than preventive, treatment. This preoccupation is behind much of the reluctance on the part of the public to seek routine help, in the absence of acute injury or discomfort. Indeed, if the present inadequate system is flooded with patients who are newly able to get the help they have always needed, because some kind of insurance will pay the bills, it is fairly predictable that the medical profession will react by becoming far more intolerant of the patient with minor or perhaps imaginary complaints than it is now.

A second failing the citizens' board found is that screening programs for identifying illnesses, particularly among the poor, do not exist in sufficient numbers to discover symptoms and reverse the course of an illness before it becomes obvious through pain or disorder, by which time it may be in an acute or a chronic stage. It is clear that a mere insurance scheme will do little about this.

Third, few young doctors are attracted to rural and small-town America, so older doctors, not as well trained in new techniques, must spread themselves over wide areas. This is well known, but perhaps not so well known is what the citizens' board found further, and I quote: "Where attempts have been made to broaden the range of choice and reduce the dependence on doctors, the medical profession has often resisted. Arkansas, for example, has established a midwife training and licensing program. . . . A doctor's signature on a card is required by law for midwife deliveries. If the patient has money, the doctor won't sign the card even if the delivery would be safe for a midwife. If the patient can't pay, the card gets signed."

Fourth, there is the problem residents of the inner cities have, like that of rural citizens. There are few doctors in their neighborhoods, and most of those there are older practitioners who have been there for years and are forced to spread themselves too thinly in an effort to deal with the massive need for their help. Many inner-city residents are poor, so their neighborhood does not promise a young doctor a lucrative practice, and further, there is a high incidence of crime in these areas which discourages doctors from opening offices or purchasing homes. No comment is necessary on the fact that an insurance plan will leave this problem untouched.

Fifth, the board found that state and federal programs have had little effect on opening up minimum health services to the poor. This is particularly true when hospital care is needed, since many private hospitals reserve most of their in-patient beds for doctors with staff privileges, and the poor do not usually have access to such doctors.

Another problem the board found is that the increase in specialization of medical practice has confused many people. They do not understand which doctor is needed for their particular problem, or whether a specialist is indeed necessary.

All of these shortcomings are the result of one root cause: the fee-for-service basis of our health system. As long as the nation permits doctors to run the show, that system will not work. Health policy—the organization and delivery of medical services—must be formulated and administered by public bodies, from federal to local, which are responsive to the needs of the public and not protective of the profit and prerogatives of physicians. We have been victimized far too long by the medieval mystery approach to medicine that the profession has fostered and honored. Each of us has been taught to dream, when we think of medical care, of someone exactly like the physician portrayed on television by Robert Young. Dr. Marcus Welby is wise, kind, selfless, skillful, dedicated—in short, superhuman. I have never met a superhuman doctor, and I am sure none exists, but somehow the medical profession has succeeded in wrapping itself in a supernatural cloak that makes the meanest of its members seem grand.

It is time to clear our eyes of this illusion and get rid of Dr. Welby once and for all. There is no mystery about medicine and surgery. Most of its practitioners are quite ordinary people, with severe limitations of skill. Most of what a doctor does can be done by any intelligent person who has been properly trained. As long as we think, when we try to meet our health needs, of somehow covering the country with a network of Dr. Welbys—as the medical profession has brainwashed us into thinking—our health needs will not be met.

In real life, Dr. Welby is not much interested in preventive medicine, such as getting rid of the lead-based paint that has poisoned fully one-third of the children growing up in older city housing. He does not want to see the quantity and quality of paraprofessionals increased and jealously surrounds their licensing procedures with thorny restrictions. If he has anything to do with a black lung victim, his contact is restricted to ordering an X-ray and filling out a form for the Social Security Administration. He does not see as his concern the shocking coal dust conditions in which coal miners work and contract black lung.

At the beginning of the nineteenth century, education was provided for our citizens very much as health care is provided now. It was a service provided for a fee. The majority of Americans who did not have the fee, did not get the service. More than a hundred years ago, we decided that universal free public education was the only system appropriate to a democracy. Not to mince words, we socialized our schools. Since then, private education has been permitted—under government control, at least in the more progressive states—but our main effort has been put into the development and operation of the public school system. In medicine, by contrast, the public health system has been a stepchild while the private system has dominated everything. We have never seen health as a right. It has been conceived as a privilege, available only to those who can afford it. This is the real reason the American health care system is in such a scandalous state.

No reasonable person—no practical politician—could propose at this point such a thorough, radical reform as would be involved in a complete government takeover of the system at one stroke. This would be radical in the strict sense of the word. I do not shrink from the word, or from the reality. But while I can advocate such a radical step, as the ideal, what I am interested in doing is getting something done, not wasting time in an intellectual fairyland of theories and impractical programs. We must deal with the situation as it is and make what progress we can. The fact is that the doctors are in command of the medical service system. We cannot at this point expropriate them, and most Americans do not want to. What must be done is to act, with their help if possible and over their dead bodies where necessary, to do three simple things:

- Make sure that no one is denied health care because he cannot afford it. A universal national health insurance scheme will do this.

- Make sure that no one is denied health care because it is not available. This will take a massive national effort to increase our output of medical professionals of every type, and a considerable degree of public regulation of how and where these new professionals are used. The inner city and the remote countryside must be served, whether it is accomplished by persuasion or by coercion.

- These two basics accomplished, we must develop a health service system that is oriented toward producing and preserving health, not simply providing medical care for illness and injury. This will require as much concern with the environment—lead paint in old apartments, poison in our streams and air, coal dust in the mines—as with the traditional aspects of medicine. Nutrition from before birth through old age would be one of the major elements of a really effective health system: the nutritionists would be the stars of the show and not, as now, supporting players.

None of what I have said is utopian. I am not proposing any miracles. All it would take is a new attitude toward health—that it is a human right, not a privilege to be purchased—and a determination to organize our government on every level to give the right to health the priority that it deserves, alongside or even ahead of the priorities of education and full employment. Can we afford it? We can easily afford it if we devote our energy to human needs and stop the diversion of our resources to such inhuman goals as war, the exploration of other planets, the protection of rich oilmen and big farmers, and the rest of the anti-social and inhuman uses to which our government has been put.

INDEX